TRAWLER TRASH

A Nautical Novel by

Ed Robinson

TRAWLER
TRASH

*Confessions
of a Boat Bum*

This is dedicated to my daughter, Alison.
She's the best thing I ever had a part in creating.

AUTHOR'S DISCLAIMER

This is a work of fiction. Real people and actual places are used fictitiously. Although some of the events described are loosely based on my true life experience, they are mostly products of my imagination.

I leave it to the reader to sort out truth from fiction.

PRELUDE

T HE NAME'S BREEZE, MEADE EDWIN Breeze to be exact. Everyone has called me Breeze since I put on my first baseball uniform in high school. Having your last name on the back of your jersey was a big step towards manhood in those days. Robbie became Rob, Donnie became Don, and Coach Everett called us all by our last names.

The name suited me. I breezed through high school, never studying for a minute. I played some good ball. I had some great girlfriends. I discovered beer. College was more of the same carefree living. I loved being called Breeze. Life was free and the living was easy. Those days are long gone now.

I never once stopped to think how life might change for me. I assumed that the future would automatically supply me with easy opportunities. I thought the fun would go on forever. I thought life would be the breeze that it had always been for me. Boy was I was wrong.

Every once in a while life hangs a curveball and I knock it out of the park. Much more often life blows me away with fastballs that I can't catch up to. Rare hits are far overshadowed by strikeout after strikeout.

I am a loser.

RUNNING FROM THE MAN

WAS SITTING UNDER THE GAZEBO at the end of C-Dock at Fisherman's Village Marina, in Punta Gorda, Florida. Colorado Bob and Kentucky Tom were letting me pilfer beers out of their coolers. These were my last two friends on Earth. They were two of the few who knew how broke and desperate I really was.

Tom drank Budweiser, which I really didn't like much. He also bore a strange resemblance to Beevis, from Beevis and Butthead. He had a self-deprecating wit and was always willing to lend a hand when needed. He was also a diver. I used him to clean the boat's hull and he never charged me full price, sometimes doing it in exchange for my homemade rum, which he fed to his wife to keep her docile. Wherever Tom was, so too was his dog Truman. In fact, he planned his bar stops and special events based on how dog-friendly the place was. Me and Truman were cool. Bob had Yuengling in his cooler, which suited me much better. I alternated beers from each, though, to keep the ledger even. Once I made a score, I'd come back with a case of Busch Lite and we'd all share. Bob had a fine gentlemen's appearance. He was always neatly groomed and sharply dressed. You couldn't pass by his boat without him offering you a beer.

"When are you going to have another batch of rum?" asked Bob. "I'm almost out." Bob liked his rum. He's the only person I've ever known that mixes rum with tonic.

"Another week or so and I can hook you up." I reminded him I needed his empty bottles to refill. Then I turned to Tom. "You drown that crazy wife of yours yet?"

That's when we saw him coming down the dock. He was not a tourist. He wasn't a boater either. He was wearing dress pants and shiny black shoes. His dark sunglasses didn't say Florida. They said agent of some kind. His plain, white, tailored shirt was sweating through. I looked my drinking buddies in the eye and said, "Follow my lead."

I always assumed they'd come after me some day. I didn't know if it would be police or the IRS, but they would come. There was no way to tell who this guy worked for, and he did not identify himself. Instead, he walked right up to our table and put his hands down on it. "Have any of you gentlemen seen one Meade Breeze around here lately?"

I spoke up first before Tom or Bob could blow it. "Breeze hasn't been around here in over a year. Haven't seen or heard from him in a long time."

If he was looking for me, I'm sure he had seen a picture. His trouble was that I had lost about forty pounds and grown my hair out long since that picture was taken. He raised his glasses and gave me a squinty once-over. I shrugged. "You got a card or something in case we see him?"

"No," he answered. "I'll be back." With that he turned and started heading back up the dock towards the parking lot. Halfway to the end of the dock he stopped. He turned around and looked back our way, rubbing his chin. He sensed something was wrong here, at least, that's what I was thinking. His indecision saved me.

"Later, guys," I yelled as I ran the other way. My dinghy was tied up at the end of D-Dock. Mystery man yelled for me to stop but it was futile. I'm no track athlete, but my head start was too much. I untied old Patches and fired up the Mercury on the first pull. The old outboard didn't let me down this time. Starting on the first pull was about a fifty-fifty proposition. Hell, sometimes starting at all was questionable.

My pursuer stood at the end of D-Dock taking pictures of me with his cell phone. I knew that once I made it to the other side of Harpoon Harry's he wouldn't be able to see me anymore. My boat was anchored just outside the canal to the Isles Yacht Club, less than a mile away. I needed to weigh anchor and make myself scarce before he could commandeer a boat and come after me. I had no idea how bad he wanted to catch me. I didn't even know which agency he was with. All I knew was that The Man had found me.

I was really feeling the adrenaline as I raced across a shallow flat towards safety. I laughed out loud at the absurdity of my situation. I'd like to be a fly on the wall when that guy tells his superior that his suspect escaped via dinghy. Coming within a hundred yards of my trawler, I eased off the throttle to bring the little boat down off plane. That's when it happened. With a cough and a sputter the old Mercury died.

"Shit," I hollered out loud. I kicked the empty five-gallon gas can that I had intended to fill while at the marina. I was out of gas. I made a lousy fugitive. This new development sobered me up pretty quick. I dropped the oars and started rowing before I lost all forward momentum. Inflatable boats don't row very well and I was fighting a combination of wind and current. I took a glance back and saw no one in pursuit. I stroked like a madman anyway. Angling the oars deeper I pulled my little boat as if it was in an Olympic competition. I punished myself for being so lax in my personal security. I was going to have to be much more careful in the future. I was a wanted man after all.

Eventually, I was able to reach out and grab the swim platform and haul myself aboard the bigger boat. There was no time to break down and stow the dinghy, so I tied off a long painter and prepared to take it in tow. I fired up the tired Lehman 120 diesel and jogged up to the bow to raise the anchor. I made mental calculations as to how much fuel I had in the tanks. Pulling up the anchor was a major pain the ass. My windlass has ceased to operate years ago. Hand over hand I hauled up the chain and fed it into the anchor locker. By the time I was finished I was drenched in sweat, and my hands were raw from stray barnacles and sand. *Mental note to self: wear gloves, you idiot.*

I wondered what else I was forgetting as I climbed the ladder to the fly-bridge. My little close call was affecting my thinking ability. *Breathe, Breeze. Settle down.* There would be plenty of time to gather my thoughts on this trip. My old trawler traveled at a stately six knots. It would be nearly four hours before I could nudge her into my hidey hole near Pelican Bay. I needed that time to formulate some kind of plan. Cash was low. Food stores were low. I didn't get a chance to take on water like I had planned. The tanks were maybe half full.

I piloted the old trawler out of the Peace River, around Whorehouse Point and turned her south towards marker five. I tried to take stock of my overall situation. Things were pretty dire without this mystery man coming so close. I chuckled to myself about trying to run in such a slow boat. Six knots wouldn't win a turtle race. Slow and steady old girl, just keep chugging like you always do.

We made the turn at marker five, off Cape Haze, and Boca Grande came into view. Soon I could make out the shoreline of Cayo Costa. I realized I was really thirsty. Having my free beer-drinking session interrupted, and followed by a vigorous rowing session had left me dying of thirst. Normally I'd hoard any beers I had aboard but I felt I deserved a few at that moment. It was times like these that I wished I had bought an autopilot when I had the money. By the time I climbed down the ladder, grabbed a beer out of the fridge, and climbed back up, we were way off course.

In my mind I told *Miss Leap* that she should know the way by now. Her real name was *Leap of Faith* but I always referred to her as *Miss Leap*. Whenever we completed a journey, I'd pat her on the transom and tell her she did a good job. She was a 1980 Blue Seas Yacht. She sported the Europa style, with overhangs around the sides and over the aft deck. Her lines were all class, but she was aging. At first I had kept her pristine, constantly caring for her teak and gel coat. I couldn't afford that these days. She didn't appear derelict, or anything; it was just that the first signs of neglect were becoming apparent. From a distance, people thought her a beauty. Upon closer inspection, they'd see the oxidation and cracking varnish. She was my home. Without her I'd be just like the bums in the park.

A few miles remained until we entered Pelican Pass. The sun was about to set over the Boca Grande Pass. The water closer to the Gulf had turned blue. I sat at the helm with my precious beer and watched the water become inflamed with the image of the sunburned sky. I had a moment of happiness in an otherwise miserable life. The beauty of my surroundings was often the only thing that kept me going. I had lost everything I had ever loved except for this old boat. I had screwed up royally thereafter. I had no future, but I kept on living.

Now it looked like the endgame was getting near. I had no choice but to keep running, keep hiding. The years of freedom that living on a boat had provided made the prospect of jail seem a certain death sentence. I shook myself out of this introspection as we approached the entrance channel to Pelican Bay. Normally I'd anchor in the open bay. I had to stay off the mangroves to avoid the mosquitoes. This time would be different.

I passed the sand spit to starboard and turned off towards the park service docks. Veering south, I left the other anchored boats in my quiet wake and angled towards a cut in the bar that would allow me entrance to a mostly-hidden cove. I slowed to a crawl in case I hit bottom. If you did this right there was plenty of water, but the cut was narrow. During the day you could see the bar to port and the grass bed to starboard. I arrived after sunset and had to rely on my GPS only. We made it through without a bump and I dropped anchor about an hour after dark. I spent the rest of the night just sitting and staring at the moon as it rose in the sky. How in the hell had I ever let my life spiral so far downward? Finally, I gave up on thinking and hit the bunk with the smell of *Off* prominent on my skin and the odor of despair coming from my soul.

THE LOVELY LAURA

ONCE UPON A TIME, I lived a charmed life. The highlight of my existence was my marriage to Laura. She was a tall thin blonde whose life force shone like an aura. We were deeply in love and happier together than I ever thought possible. Life had been a cakewalk for me. I always had the prettiest girls, the fast track in my career, a horseshoe up my ass. Whatever I touched turned to gold. Though I didn't go to church and wasn't particularly religious, every night I'd send a silent "thank you" to God for all of my blessings.

Laura was the culmination of a life of good fortune. We shared an intimacy that I hadn't known with previous lovers. We shared common goals, one of which was to live on a boat in paradise. We both had wonderful jobs. The money flowed in and we had everything we could ever want. Mostly, we had each other. When I told her that I'd be there until the light died in her eyes, I meant it with all of my heart. She became my world, and I hers.

Tragically, I was there when the light died in her eyes. I would have given my own life to take her place, but God had different plans for me. Laura had suffered a lower back injury and subsequently was diagnosed with a rare pain disorder. The doctors decided that epidural injections with a steroid solution would treat the problem. It didn't help. As time passed she got worse and worse. They pumped her up with narcotics to ease the pain. She was slowly drifting away. Then one day when I came into her room I was intercepted by the nurse. During the night she had suffered a stroke and was now paralyzed. She was on a ventilator, and a dialysis machine, and a vast assortment of tubes and wires ran to various gizmos by her bed.

Eventually, we learned that a placed called the New England Compounding Center had sent out a contaminated batch of methylprednisolone acetate steroid injections. The Center for Disease Control reported that one hundred and thirty-seven people were infected with fungal meningitis. Twelve of those people died. You may have heard about it in the news. Laura was one of those people.

That moment in time when she breathed her last, something snapped inside me. I held her lifeless body in my arms and wailed like a baby. I rocked her back and forth and patted her back and squeezed her like I'd never let go. Nurses and doctors gave me a bit of time, but eventually they led me away. I stood like a zombie in the waiting room, not comprehending what had just happened. A nurse's aide asked if I needed anything. Could she call me a cab? I just shook my head no, and shuffled out into the night.

I found my truck, but I couldn't drive. Until that night I hadn't cried since high school. I had broken up with my first love and bawled my eyes out on the walk home. Janet Wiggins was so sweet. We had shared all our firsts together. Her family was so kind to me. Why did I do it? There was a new girl in town who I thought was super hot. Cynthia Riffe agreed to date me. It was fun, but it didn't last long. I regretted what I'd done to Janet. It wouldn't be the last choice in life that I'd regret.

Afterwards, I watched my mother die from cancer. I was stoic. I took care of her affairs in a cool and professional manner. Then my sister died too. No tears were shed, even though I would miss her dearly. Finally, my father passed away. He was a great man whom I admired, but I kept my grief in check. This time was different. I simply could not wrap my brain around Laura's death. I cried all night lying on the seat of my truck. I couldn't stop. Waves of heart-crushing grief swept over me. I was practically paralyzed with the pain. I felt it deep in my soul.

The next morning I managed to drive home. I left the radio off for fear that a song would play that would set me off. When I opened the door to our home it hit me all over again. She was everywhere in that house, except she was gone. I struggled to come to terms with my weakness. I simply couldn't function. There were things I was supposed to do, but I couldn't think of what they were or how I would do them. Our favorite song kept haunting me. *"I'll be there, 'til the light, dies in your eyes."* Oh God, how could you let this happen?

I took the fifth of rum out of the freezer where we kept it. We had a ritual of doing shots together. I set out two shot glasses and filled them both. I raised my glass in the air and made a toast to the lovely Laura. I slammed it down and left her glass full. I took the bottle with me into the living room and proceeded to drink in down. I laid back in my big leather recliner and stared at the ceiling, waiting for the rum to ease my pain. The phone rang and rang but went unanswered. I had no idea how I was ever going to carry on without Laura. I couldn't even bear to consider it. I let the booze cloud my mind until I drifted off.

In the morning I realized I needed to perform a few simple tasks, like eating. I also needed to call my boss. I thought I should probably call someone to help me, but just didn't think I could handle having anyone around. I found Laura's shot glass still full on the counter, so I picked it up and drank it down. This allowed me a moment of clarity. I used it to turn on the laptop and email my boss with a brief explanation and ask for some leave time. I recalled suddenly that it was Laura's wish to be cremated. My old friend Wells Faries had taken her from the hospital. I shot him an email as well. I asked that he let me know when I could pick up Laura's ashes. I then sent out a mass text to all my contacts informing them of her death. I asked that I be left alone. I didn't want visitors or phone calls anytime soon. That was all I could handle that day. For ten minutes I fought to concentrate so I could do what was needed. Then the grief pulled me down once again.

I spent the rest of the week drinking rum and wallowing in my misery. I alternated between sorrow and anger, anger at God. Laura was the finest human being I'd ever had the pleasure to meet in this world. Now she was gone at age forty seven. God is one cruel bastard, I thought. *Screw you, God. What's the point?*

At times I reached hysteria, screaming to the heavens, saying all sorts of vile things. Other times I lay down on the floor and whimpered. I punched a few holes in the drywall. I pounded my fists on the floor and cried, "NOOOO!" My mind raced all over the place. Memories of Laura, my job responsibilities, moving on, how would I cope with my future? The only thing that helped was the rum. When I ran out I'd drive to the next town to restock so no one would see me. I hadn't shaved or showered in a week. I barely ate.

On day eight I checked my email again to see hundreds of messages. Sifting through I saw that my boss wanted to know when I'd return to work. I also saw that I could pick up Laura's ashes at any time. Those two things I dreaded. I left the other emails unread and went to take a shower. I told myself I'd have to snap out of it and face the world sooner or later. When I went to shave I saw my face in the mirror. Good Lord, I was death warmed over. No food, little sleep and lots of rum had transformed me into a haggard-looking mess. Where was Breeze?

That vision of my face in the mirror was like a slap to the head. I was no longer the mighty Meade Breeze, master of my domain. All of my good fortune was worth nothing now. The charmed life had turned into a curse. I had no experience with this. God and the universe had coddled me all my life. I wasn't prepared to be hit so hard. Fate had blindsided me and it looked like I was down for the count. *Pull yourself together, Breeze. At least pretend you're okay.*

After I got cleaned up I picked up the phone and called my boss. Bob Zola and I had been friends and coworkers for a long time. He knew Laura well and was a very understanding person. I could talk to him. "Bob, I'm picking up Laura's ashes today and I'll be back to work on Monday." He seemed relieved to hear from me. "You sure Breeze?" he asked. "Take all the time you need." "No Bob, I'm dying here. I've got to have something to do. I'll be all right." "Suit yourself," was Bob's reply. "See you on Monday."

Okay, good, Breeze. Call Wells. Wells had the local funeral home in town and had helped with the loss of my parents and sister. I could never do his job, but he was damned good at it. "Wells, it's Breeze. Can I stop by today to pick up the ashes?"

"Sure, Breeze, anytime before five, and I'm really sorry for your loss."

I apologized for not getting back to him sooner, and hung up. He said he understood. As I put down the phone I looked around the house and wondered what to do next. The rum was calling me, but I had committed to return to work. The grief was calling me too. I wanted to sit down and cry again but fought it. I looked around the house and wondered what to do next. The idea that I should pack up Laura's things occurred to me, but I didn't have the heart for it. Instead, I dug out our photo albums. I stacked them on the kitchen table and popped open a beer. Thumbing through our memories brought slow tears. I didn't break down and sob. I didn't lose control. Instead I continued gazing at Laura's beautiful smile. I loved that woman so much. Our life in pictures was a fine one. I dawdled on the photos of our trip to the BVI. We spent a week on a catamaran drinking beer, soaking up the sun, and making love on the

Caribbean Sea. It was there that I proposed. We were so happy then. I tried to touch her in the pictures. I stroked her hair. That week was like being in heaven. We decided afterwards that we wanted to buy a boat and live in paradise together for the rest of our days.

Right then I decided that I would follow that dream. I'd take that boat back to the BVI and spread Laura's ashes on the white sands of the islands. I didn't know how I'd make that happen, but I'd figure something out. In an instant I had found a purpose. I'd make it my life's goal to get Laura back to the islands. Not on a plane or a charter boat, but on our own vessel. My soul was still missing something. My brain wasn't really thinking properly, but I'd manufactured a reason to go on. It wouldn't be without Laura. It would be with her.

BREEZE GOES BAD

FOUR YEARS LATER I WAS still carrying that urn with Laura's ashes. I hadn't made it to the BVI. I did manage to buy a boat. I found it in Florida and christened it *Leap of Faith*. Laura and I had chosen the name back when we dreamed of sailing away together. I poured myself a glass of champagne after the christening ceremony. I poured a glass for Laura and placed it next to the urn. I listed the boat's home port as the British Virgin Islands, which was now a sad joke considering she had never left Florida.

The methods I used to finance the boat purchase and my escape from society are why I'm in so much trouble now. I had gone back to work and it hadn't gone well. There was a disconnect in my mind. The unbearable loss was a weight on my chest that threatened to crush the life out of me. Nothing mattered to me except buying a boat and running away with Laura's ashes. I didn't want to speak with customers. I didn't want to deal with my employees. My thoughts were out of control. I forgot things that were important to the job. I made poor decisions.

It became apparent that my coworkers and superiors were only tolerating me out of pity. If I thought about that too much, it disgusted me. I was embarrassed by my sudden incompetence but powerless to change. All I wanted was to escape. I needed money for that. One day, a little devil appeared on my shoulder and pointed out how easy it would be to embezzle funds from my employer.

"They trust you," the little devil said. "You've been a loyal employee for over a decade. You're in charge of the books here and there is no oversight."

He had a valid point, even though what he was suggesting was very wrong. It would be child's play to transfer funds. Of course, it would be discovered during month-end accounting, but by then I could be long gone. It was stupid, illogical, and immoral . . . but it could be done with ease. I stood at a great crossroads in my life. I stood there and weighed my choices, considering the consequences of what I was contemplating. I knew right from wrong, but

I stood there at that crossroads and chose to do the wrong thing.

That night I logged in to my 401(k) account to check the balance. I had sixty grand that I could withdraw. I knew there was a tax penalty for early withdrawal, but screw the IRS. I wouldn't pay them. Then I checked my savings account balance. There was thirty grand there. I had ninety thousand of my own money. I decided to lift another ninety from my employer.

Back at work I started paying closer attention to my duties. I also started paying closer attention to the financial accounts, looking for the smoothest way to hide my theft. I put together a plan, carefully considering the timing. I knew they would find it. I just needed a few weeks to disappear. Try finding me on a boat in the islands.

I decided to wait until tax time. The company's accountants would all be swamped and less likely to catch on to my deception. Plus, there was the fact that I wouldn't be filing my own tax forms. It seemed like an appropriate time to go on the lam. In the meantime, I sought out a lawyer to sue the hospital, doctors, pharmacy, etc. I wanted to punish everyone involved in Laura's death.

I had an acquaintance named Mike Savage that had his own small firm. It was my understanding that business was slow. I could throw him a bone, and he seemed like a nice enough guy, for a lawyer, that is. When I finished explaining my case to him, he said, "This could take years if you don't want to settle out of court. It's a slam dunk, but they'll fight it and drag it out as long as possible." I thought briefly about reconsidering my embezzlement scheme, but I couldn't wait years.

"Those bastards killed my wife, Mike. I don't want to settle. Take your time. Make them pay and I'll split it with you. I don't care how long it takes."

This raised his eyebrows. He started shuffling papers and promised to do his best.

"Just don't get impatient on this, Breeze," he said. "There'll be a chunk of change for both of us somewhere down the road."

We shook hands and I walked out of his office. I had a vague notion that someday I'd be rich, but it did nothing to lessen my grief. I decided to put the lawsuit, and its potential payday out of my mind. If it happened, it happened.

I spent my days pretending to be a good manager and employee. I spent my nights pounding rum out of the freezer and cursing the Gods. I occasionally anguished over soon becoming a criminal, but the little devil always won that argument. The time was drawing near and I still had steps to take.

On weekends I shopped for boats on the internet. I found what I wanted in Florida and called the broker. I told him I'd be down just after tax day to see the boat. I packed up Laura's clothes, delivering half to Goodwill and half to the Salvation Army. I got rid of the rest of our belongings, keeping only the photo albums and some clothes for me. I had my finger on the trigger of my scam. I knew that once that bullet was fired, there was no recalling it. I was going through with it anyway.

I think everyone has been there. What is it with human nature? Just before we do something stupid, deep inside we know that it's wrong, but we do it anyway. I know people who stood at the altar thinking, "This is the wrong decision." They got married anyway. Heroin junkies think just before that first high, "This is stupid." Then they shoot up. Petty criminals must know that robbing a liquor store is wrong, yet they do it anyway. Humans can be really stupid sometimes. I was no exception.

Just before tax day, I hid ninety thousand dollars from an account I had access to. I shuffled it around through several other accounts before transferring it to my own. It would serve as only minor confusion to any experienced auditor, but no sense making it too easy to find. As soon as I hit the final button on my keyboard, I logged off and headed home. My bag was packed and the truck was fueled. I transferred all the money to a bank in Florida under an assumed name. Don't ask how I managed to acquire it.

I had Laura's ashes, a few photo albums, and a duffel bag full of clothes. I left an empty house for whoever would find it. I left my cell phone on the counter along with the keys. As I started up the truck it felt like jumping off a cliff. There was no turning back now. All I could do was take a leap of faith. I was now a criminal. There was no way to know how long it would take before some law enforcement would actually come looking for me, or even if they would. How hard would they pursue me? Drive the speed limit, use your turn signals, and play it cool. You're just a lone traveler on his way to Florida to buy a boat.

It's hard to explain how I felt driving south on I-95 with Laura's ashes. My grief was like another passenger sitting next to me. I was driving through a tunnel with the BVI on the far end. I couldn't see it, but I knew it was there. First I'd have to deal with Florida.

I slept in the truck at a rest area the first night somewhere in South Carolina. The second night I slept in a hotel parking lot in Cocoa Beach. I walked out onto the sand in the morning to watch the sunrise. It glistened over the Atlantic Ocean and it felt like magic. I wanted to run and grab the urn from the truck so Laura could see it. I stopped myself. How weird would that be? Two days in and I'm already losing my mind. *Straighten up, Breeze. Keep your wits about you*.

On day three I made it across the state to Punta Gorda. I slept in the truck at Gilchrest Park overlooking Charlotte Harbor. I resisted the urge to hold the urn in my lap as the last of the sun's rays blinked out of sight. In the morning I noticed some homeless-looking guys going in and out of the public restroom. It appeared they were washing up in there. This was my introduction to The Bums. There was a small group of vagrants living nearby, a few of which had raggedy boats anchored off the park. Cross-Eyed John appeared to be their leader. He was the most articulate and had the nicest living accommodations. His little sailboat wasn't in too bad of shape, and he had mastered the public restroom cleanup routine. He introduced himself as JR, but all the other bums called him Cross-Eyed John. He was slight in build, possibly with some Native American blood in him. He wore his dark hair in a long braid.

He introduced me to Crazy Hank, whose boat was half sunk and missing its mast. Toothless Tim lived in his Ford Ranger in the parking lot. Others slept in the ancient banyan tree roots over by the hotel. I hadn't slept or changed clothes in three days, so they assumed I was one of them. I didn't correct this assumption, instead availing myself of the restroom to wash up a bit, shave and change clothes. I had almost two hundred thousand bucks in the bank and a broker to meet.

A NEW LIFE

L EPRECHAUN RON WORKED FOR PIER One Yacht Sales at Fisherman's Village Marina. He was a spritely little fellow with a twinkle in his eye and a constant smile. Retired from a career at West Marine, Ron knew boats. He also knew that I was not only a serious buyer, but I was also in a hurry. He sensed a nice commission and worked hard to smooth my transition from landlubber to live-aboard.

When he took me to slip C-18 right there in Fisherman's Village Marina, it was love at first sight. There floated a 1980 Oceania 36 trawler. Classic in design, she was covered in nicely finished teak. She was missing half the accessories on my want list, but I didn't care. I wanted to make an offer right there on the spot, but Ron slowed me down. I needed a surveyor first, and being less obvious about my hurry would improve my bargaining position. He really was a helpful and knowledgeable broker. We retired to the bar to plan our offer strategy. Ron paid for the beers, which further endeared me to him.

I couldn't wait to close the deal and take possession of my new boat. Soon enough we completed the survey and sea trial. All was in order and we went to closing a week later. I handed over a certified check for sixty grand, and he handed me the keys to my new home. I moved my meager possessions aboard immediately. The first order of business was to find a spot to put Laura's urn. I had the need to be able to see it. I couldn't stow it away where I might forget. She was on my mind constantly. Looking at her urn was all I had left of her. I parked her front and center on the dash above the lower helm. Each time I'd throw the lines and get underway I wrapped her in a blanket and laid her down on the settee.

I settled in to the marina life a little too nicely. These people didn't know about Laura. They didn't know I was a crook, either. I gave vague answers to questions about my past and managed to make some new friends. I got to know Colorado Bob and Kentucky Tom during our evening beer drinking sessions under the gazebo between C and D docks.

Bob was an experienced sailor who had traveled all through the Caribbean. I picked his brain about offshore navigation, anchorages, and points of interest. He was a wealth of knowledge, and a good person in general. Kentucky Tom didn't know squat about sailing, even though he had brought his boat down the inland waterways all the way from Kentucky. He made the trip without ever putting up a sail, navigating with his cell phone. He had quit his comfortable job and reasonable pay in order to move to Florida and live on a boat. Now he worked two jobs and still made less money. Both were quick to share beers and equally quick with a laugh.

I also met Big Lloyd. He lived at the far end of D-Dock on a huge motor-sailor. He was a mountain of a man with a big deep laugh and a heart of gold. His job required constant travel, so he was gone a lot. I started keeping an eye on things while he was away. He and his wife, Lynn, seemed to take a special interest in me. I enjoyed hanging out with them, except when they asked questions about where I came from or what I used to do. No one really figured out how a man so young could be living here with no visible means of support. I continued to be vague or change the subject whenever it came up. Let them think I'm a trust fund baby or an internet millionaire.

All the folks in the marina were nice to me and to each other. There was a real laid-back vibe there. I liked it. It was nothing like where I had came from. All the stresses of work and modern society were gone for me here. Hanging out at the pool drinking a margarita during the day, drinking beer on the dock while the sun went down, I took to this new life pretty quickly. I started poking around the town, checking out the bars. The Tiki Bar at the Four Points Hotel was pretty neat. It featured cheap beers, trucked-in sand, and a nice view of the sunset. Hurricane Charley's on the other side of the bridge featured great live music every night and was a premier sunset-viewing venue.

The Nav-A-Gator Grill up the Peace River was a pure old Florida cracker joint that hosted some of the best musicians in Florida every weekend. Bert's Bar in Matlacha was a funky little dive bar with a million-dollar view. They served the best grouper fingers that I could find. I made the rounds and started recognizing the same people on the circuit. I'd call these folks acquaintances rather than friends, but my social circle was growing.

I made mental notes on the single ladies. Several had been very friendly. Maybe they were interested in me? I couldn't imagine being with another woman. My heart was still full with Laura. I still hadn't come to terms with her death. I couldn't help but notice, though, when they approached and made conversation. There were some knockouts available in this town. MJ was a pretty lady, maybe a little older than me. She was nice looking, quick witted and a little reserved. She seemed like a real lady. Liz was smoking hot. She was petite with long flowing hair and a killer smile. She wasn't one to dance on tables or get sloppy drunk like some of the others. If I was looking for a partner, she'd do very nicely. Natalie was real nice too. This town was full of pretty people, though most of them were married. It was nice to go out, listen to music, and watch all the nice couples having fun.

I started doing the social scene a lot. I spent money like I had an unlimited supply. The marina was costing me almost nine hundred per month with the slip rent, electric, and live-aboard fee. Beers at some of the bars were four bucks a piece. A night out with six beers and a meal would run me forty bucks, fifty with a big tip to the server. I learned that during those three or four hours, I could let my grief slip. If I was sitting on the boat alone and forgot about Laura for ten minutes, I'd feel guilty. At the bars I had an excuse to be distracted from my grief. This went on for months. I had gotten sucked in by an easy life. I even managed to have a little fun. What I had not done was take off for the BVI. Hell, I hadn't even left the slip.

When I came to that realization, I chastised myself for losing track of my goal. I had stolen money, evaded taxes and ran away in order to return Laura's ashes to the islands. Instead I was partying it up in Punta Gorda, and generally being good for nothing. I vowed to cast off and continue my journey. I rededicated myself to the mission as if I was returning the Holy Grail to its rightful place.

I spent the next few weeks preparing *Miss Leap* for travel. In the meantime, a send-off party was being planned. The entire marina and a bunch of non-marina acquaintances met for a sunset party and a bon voyage bash in my honor. I was going to miss my new friends, especially Colorado Bob and Kentucky Tom. After we got good and stoned and most of the partygoers had left, Big Lloyd pulled me aside. I don't know if he sensed that something was amiss with my life or what. He said he was about to buy a house in Punta Gorda Isles with a deep water dock. If I ever needed a place to stay, look him up. I wasn't sure what to think about his offer. We'd only known each other for a few months, but we were growing closer by the day. I shelved it in the back of my mind, hoping I'd never have cause to take him up on it.

I was ready to leave. One bright sunny morning with no wind at all on the harbor, I untied from the dock and eased out of the marina on my way south. I anchored up in Pelican Bay that first day and explored the island in the dinghy. I found manatees to play with and dolphins to chase. Tarpon rolled in the clear waters of the Gulf. I sat on the beach and looked out over all the blue. I could stay here forever, but I had something to take care of first.

I spent a few days there getting used to living at anchor. I learned to conserve water. I learned not to waste electricity. I went without a real shower. I had no one to impress. Next stop was Fort Myers Beach. I took a mooring ball which entitled me to a real, hot shower. I also got rid of my trash and picked up a few more things from the grocery store. You can take the dinghy right up to the market here, which I thought was cool. I made a mental note of that tidbit for possible future use.

I walked into town, and what did I find? I saw bar after bar lining both sides of the street. I heard live music wafting up into the night air. I couldn't resist. I had one beer at the Smoking Oyster Brewery. I drank another at the Yucatan Beach Stand. I had one at the Japanese place across the street. I went beer for beer with almost every bar on the strip until I feared I wouldn't be able to walk back to the dinghy dock. I made it all the way down to the Lani Kai where I found hundreds of college kids drinking like there was no tomorrow. The place was filthy. The bathrooms were disgusting. There was puke in the elevator. There were also a hundred or more tight, bikini bodies in a drunken stupor. I sat and watched for an hour, nursing one beer. The downstairs bar spilled out onto the beach where a volleyball game was underway. I was thirty years older than the crowd, so I was ignored. I saw topless displays and moon shots. I saw naked girls drinking Jell-O shots.

Those kids were having one hell of a party. They had no idea they were being watched by a felon. They cared not for white-collar crime or tax evasion. They weren't thinking about their future. All they had on their minds was booze and sex. It took me back to my college days, back when I was the mighty Breeze. Back then I was the big man on campus, had the prettiest girl in school, and an unlimited future. Oh, how the mighty have fallen. Now I had an old trawler and a criminal past. I had less than a hundred grand in the bank, way less, actually. I was the caretaker of an urn full of ashes. What would I do once my mission was complete?

I didn't like that question one bit, so I refocused on my travel agenda. Next stop was Marco Island. This called for my very first offshore passage. I wasn't really nervous but there was the element of the unknown facing me. The boat was running well and all systems seemed to be in order. I motored out of the Matanzas Pass at sunrise and turned south once again. Out on the Gulf waters I tried to concentrate my mind on my duties ahead. It was a long way to the islands from the west coast of Florida. I was a novice captain. The boat was old. Could this be done?

The trip went just fine. The weather was perfect. I made the thirty-six mile leg in six hours. I had a choice of two anchorages. I could take the winding, tricky channel into Smokehouse Bay. There was a Winn Dixie there if I needed it. Or I could drop anchor in the closer and easier Factory Bay. There was no way to get to shore there, but I chose it anyway. I'd leave at first light, and I didn't really need anything from the store. The high-rise condos blocked my view of the last of the sunset. That made me decide I didn't like Factory Bay. In the morning, I pulled up an anchor that was covered in thick, black mud. It made a mess of my bow and me. That made me decide I didn't much like Marco Island at all.

The trip to Little Shark River took ten hours. It was another good weather day and I spent a lot of time daydreaming about life in the islands. I conveniently ignored the fact that I'd run out of money one day. I was hiding from reality. Get to the BVI. Spread Laura's ashes. That was all the future I cared to think about. I approached the shoreline looking for the entrance to the river. There was one green marker on the chart that I needed to locate. The background scenery on shore was all green mangroves. I slowed and pulled out my binoculars to scan the horizon. *There it is. Nice and easy Breeze*. I steered *Miss Leap* carefully into a basin just inside the river entrance. I dropped anchor dead-center in the basin and backed down on it. Once settled I took a look around. This place had a prehistoric look and feel to it. No humans were in sight. Giant sea turtles rose for a breath.

Huge spotted rays glided around the boat. I saw hundred-pound tarpon roll near a creek entrance.

I thought this would be a good spot to hide someday. That was until the mosquitoes arrived. I was sitting on the aft deck with a beer, waiting for sunset, when it happened. A large black cloud came into view. It was accompanied by a buzzing noise that I couldn't make out. It was mesmerizing until I realized what it was. Millions of bloodthirsty mosquitoes were descending on the boat. I screamed and spilled my beer, scrambling into the salon. I slammed the door behind me and fished through the cabinet, looking for bug spray. A few dozen of the bastards had made it inside with me. I sprayed myself then sprayed the interior of the cabin. I choked on the fog I had created. Spraying them didn't kill them, it just pissed them off. I swatted myself all over while trying to find a fly swatter. I grabbed it and started smacking bugs all over the interior of the boat. Each direct hit left a little blood splatter on the ceiling and walls. I decided hiding out here probably wasn't such a good idea. I spent a sleepless night with my head under a blanket even though it was ninety degrees in the boat. I heard an occasional buzzing near my ears, just enough to keep me awake.

I couldn't wait to get out of this hellhole the next morning. I pulled anchor before sunup and followed my GPS track back out into the Gulf. The most direct routes to start a crossing to the Bahamas were either to Marathon or Islamorada. On the other hand, Key West wasn't much further. It wasn't in the direction I needed to go, though. Here I was again at a crossroads. Key West was the wrong choice. *Stop being stupid, Breeze.* I chose Marathon. I was proud of myself for resisting temptation.

I ran about three miles offshore before turning south. My research told me to stay well off the shoals at Cape Sable, on the southern tip of mainland Florida. I settled in for the eight or nine hour crossing of Florida Bay. My thoughts drifted back to Laura. I had an urge to go down and get the urn and bring it up on the fly bridge with me. I needed to be vigilant at the wheel, though. I shook off that thought and tried to concentrate on piloting my craft.

That's when it happened.

I heard and felt a thump under *Miss Leap's* keel. Something hard and heavy bumped and rolled under her hull. I reached to shift into neutral but I was too late. With a sickening sound of metal on metal the engine came to an abrupt stop. I was adrift in the Gulf of Mexico with no idea how much damage had just been done. *Keep your cool, Breeze. Don't panic. Stay calm and assess the situation.*

I was a mediocre swimmer at best, but I did have snorkel gear. I donned my mask and tied a line around my waist. Slipping off the swim platform, I was aware of the up-and-down motion of the boat as she rolled beam-to in the soft rollers. I'd need to be mindful of that. No need to have thirty-two thousand pounds of old boat come down on my head in the middle of nowhere.

The visibility was excellent. What I saw below the waves was not. The big prop was mangled, and the shaft appeared to be bent. Not good. As I climbed back up on the swim platform, a deep dread came over me. Was she taking on water? I quickly scrambled to open up the hatch to the bilge. I did see some water, but the pumps appeared to be keeping up with it. I got a flashlight for a closer look and found the stuffing box leaking at a pretty good clip. The shaft had pulled out a few inches. A few revolutions after it was bent would have damaged the packing. Lord knows what else would be affected.

I hung my head for a few seconds trying to figure out what to do next. I had no cell phone reception here, nor Wi-Fi. My only way to reach out to the world was on the VHF radio. I did have towing insurance through Boat US. I hailed them on channel sixteen. There was no reply. I hailed three more times before giving up. I was too far away from anyone who might hear me. Then I remembered the Coast Guard. They had tremendous range on their radios. "Sécurité, Sécurité, Sécurité.

This is the motor vessel *Leap of Faith*, dead in the water, approximately four miles west of Cape Sable. "

"Vessel hailing Coast Guard, this is the United States Coast Guard, Key West, Florida. What is the nature of your emergency?"

"I hit something with my prop and I'm dead in the water. Can you relay to Boat US please."

"Are there any injuries and is your vessel taking on water?"

"No injuries. I am taking on a small amount of water, but the pumps are keeping up, so far."

"Roger that. Stand by while we contact Boat US."

A few minutes passed before the operator advised me that a tow boat was en route from Key Largo. I kept checking the bilge to monitor the water level. It was not rising, but the main bilge pump was running constantly. I didn't feel like my life was in danger, but I worried about the condition of poor old *Miss Leap*. I had no idea how much a new prop and shaft would cost. I had no idea what other damage might have happened. I had no idea how long it would take the tow boat to get to me from Key Largo. I was pretty much out of ideas. I had finally escaped the soft life in the marina. I had finally resolved to continue my quest. Now I was just floating, disabled in the Gulf of Mexico. My destiny was undetermined.

THE VORTEX OF MARATHON

I T WAS ALMOST A THREE hour wait before the tow boat came into view. The captain threw a pair of oversized fenders over and pulled up alongside. He tossed me a line and after I secured it to a cleat he asked for my membership card. Boat US is cheap insurance. Don't leave home without it. I told him what happened and what damage I had discovered so far.

"Where you wanna go?" he asked. "I can get you anywhere from Key Largo to Marathon. Not enough daylight for anywhere else."

"I was headed to Marathon. What can you tell me about the boatyard there?"

"They do good work, can fix whatever's wrong, but you'll pay dearly," he told me.

I asked him what other options I had. He told me that there were several cheaper yards in

Islamorada and Largo, but he couldn't vouch for their quality of work.

"You want it done cheap and fast," he said. "I'll take you to Largo. You want it done right, and not in a hurry, we'll go to Marathon."

That decided it for me. I wanted it done right, and wasn't in any particular hurry. "Take me to Marathon."

He took *Miss Leap* in tow and we headed south at the same six knots I normally traveled. He let me ride with him and we chatted some to break the boredom. He was a younger guy, maybe thirty five. I heard about his past as a charter boat captain and how he had moved boats for Viking out of Tampa. He got burned out easily, he said. This job was even getting old. He hated the long tows like this one. It would be six hours or more before we made it to Boot Key Harbor, then a few more hours to get back home to Key Largo. I made a mental note to give him a nice tip once he cut me loose.

Pulling into the channel and under the bridge was a relief. My old boat, my house, everything I owned, was still floating. Mitch, the towboat man, handled the transfer expertly. The guys at the yard had me on the lift with no problems whatsoever. I thought this was a good start. They'd obviously taken boats from a tow for haul-out many times. I shook hands with Mitch, slipped him fifty bucks, and said my goodbyes. As I walked up to the yard office I wondered where he'd find work next.

Howie was the yard boss. He was a stocky, dark man with slicked-back dark hair. Gold chains hung from his neck; one of them looked like a Spanish coin from the wreck of the Atocha. Howie had a real bad back and didn't work on the boats anymore, he just supervised. In short order I learned that he was a former fire fighter. He had fought for disability for many years with no resolution, so here he was, still working even though it was killing him. He sometimes used a New Jersey Italian accent, but it was just part of his shtick. He was really from Boston.

"We was supposed to be closed an hour ago," Howie informed me. "If it wasn't good ol' Mitch calling in with a tow, you woulda missed us. He brings us lots of work, though, so we waited for you."

"I'm forever grateful, Howie. Can someone take a look at my boat in the morning?"

I then listened to a long list of other jobs that were ahead of me, how much money they were going to bring in, and how busy everybody was.

I told Howie that I lived on the boat, and I'd be hanging around his yard until it was fixed. He scratched his ass and squinted at me. He started shaking his head no. "You ain't supposed to sleep on your boat here in this yard." I slipped him a hundred dollar bill and got a stern warning. I could stay, but no trouble. I was to keep a low profile.

"The last thing I'm looking for is trouble, Howie. Low profile is my middle name. Yup, just call me Meade Low Profile Breeze." If he only knew...

He chuckled and said he had to go and lock up. He'd let me know when someone could look at my boat. The yard guys were finished putting it on jack stands and were headed for their cars. I walked over and asked one of them where I could get a cold beer and something to eat for a reasonable price. Three of them answered at once with Dorado's Dockside. That was a good enough endorsement for me.

Then I realized that my dinghy was up on the boat, which was up in the air on stands. As the yard guys drove off I hollered about a ladder. They kept on driving but pointed over to a shed with several ladders propped up against it. I spent the next hour wrestling the roughly hundred-pound little boat down to the ground. Then I dragged it across the stone work area to the pit. I hung it over the edge and slid it down to the water, tying it off to a piling. Next up was the outboard motor. It weighed about eighty-five pounds and was unwieldy. I rigged up some ropes to a little block and tackle I had on the back of the top deck and lowered it gingerly to the ground. No way was I carrying it across the lot. I searched the yard until I found a dock cart. That made transporting it simple, but I still had to get it down into the dinghy. I climbed back up onto the boat, removed the block, and took it down to where the dinghy was floating. I got a big lag bolt and hammered it and screwed it into the piling. I rigged up some rope as a harness, and lifted it off the ground. Holding onto the rope as I climbed down into the dinghy, I slowly lowered the outboard until I could grab it. I was drenched in sweat at this point, with two busted knuckles. I climbed up the ladder once again and returned with the gas tank and a life jacket. I always followed all the safety rules. I didn't want something silly like not having a life vest bring me to the attention of any law enforcement agency. I even had a little portable white light for nighttime running, and a whistle.

My contrary old Mercury did not start on the first pull. It didn't start on the second pull either. I squeezed the ball a few times. I pumped the primer a few times. I pulled the cord a few more times. I was sweating again. I was tired and thought about giving up and crawling back aboard. My thirst for a cold beer won out. I yanked the cord a dozen more times and it finally coughed to life. I threw it in gear before it could quit and putted off in search of Dorado's Dockside. I weaved in and out of the mooring field looking at all the boats. I found Dockside on the opposite side of the harbor well to the north of the boatyard. It was surrounded by dozens of dinghies of all shapes, sizes and conditions.

As I approached the dock, I heard music, good music. I climbed up and entered the bar. I expected all heads to turn but no one paid me any attention. All the tables were full with boating types. This was the local live-aboard bar apparently, which suited me just fine. Everyone was enjoying the music, drinking and eating. The place had an island vibe to it. Tiki gods adorned the deck. The decorations were all nautically themed. I liked it.

I found an empty barstool and was immediately greeted by my bartender, Carol. She caught my eye immediately. She was a medium-sized blonde. She didn't have the most gorgeous face, or the most perfect body, but the whole package was quite attractive. She was prettier than the sum of her parts. Something about her eyes kept drawing me in.

"What'll you have, sailor?" she chimed. I asked for a cold Landshark and a menu. She was back in flash with a beaming smile. She really was a nice looking gal. I couldn't pin down her age. I guessed mid-forties, but she could have been ten years younger or older. Throughout the course of the night I learned that she was married. She and her husband Miles lived aboard their sailboat *Crew Zen*. She tended bar and he was a boat mechanic here in the harbor. He worked for himself picking up whatever odd marine repair jobs came his way. He came in later and I was taken aback at how good looking he was. Tall and chiseled, he was like a male model with grease under his fingernails. They made a great couple. Both of them were as friendly as they could be. They were really at ease with themselves and the lifestyle they had chosen. Good for them. I was anything but at ease, and I was starting to seriously question my lifestyle choices.

Meanwhile, the guys playing music were sounding great. Carol told me the singer was Eric Stone, and that he owned the bar. The guitar player that night was his buddy Steve Hall, who lived on his sailboat too. They played island songs and sailing songs and they were damned good. I really appreciated their soothing sound. I can barely play the radio but I know good music when I hear it.

At one point I looked down at myself and frowned at how dirty I was. I had sweated through my clothes more than once that day. I hadn't shaved or taken a real shower since I left Fort Myers Beach. As I surveyed the bar, I realized that half the patrons were in similar shape. Wrinkled tee-shirts and four day beards seemed to be standard attire in this joint.

Eventually my fatigue overcame my buzz and I decided it was time to go. I tipped Carol a twenty and she gave me a mischievous wink. Was it flirting? She was married for crying out loud. Probably she had the whole flirty bartender thing down in order to maximize tips. I was in the Keys though. I suppose anything was possible. I put it out of my mind and set out in the dark through the harbor and back to my boat.

When I woke the next morning, I was completely disoriented. Where the hell was I? I looked out and realized I was on land. It was an odd feeling not being on the water. I began to recall the ordeal that had been yesterday. Twenty-four hours ago I was swatting mosquitoes in the Everglades. So much had happened since then. I needed coffee. I needed a shower too, but the coffee was more important. I hit the button to turn on my inverter and got nothing. The batteries were dead. The constant running of the bilge pump during our long tow must have drained them. I'd have to see Howie about shore power. It would probably cost me another hundred. I started my little Honda generator in order to get the coffee pot going. I took a cup out on the aft deck and looked over my surroundings. Instead of dolphins swimming by, I saw yard workers starting their day. Then I remembered that *Miss Leap* was crippled. It hurt me to think about it. Me and this old tub were pretty close. She was all I had.

Then my thoughts turned to Laura. She was never far from my mind, but last night at Dockside I didn't think about her once. I felt ashamed of that, so I went and got her urn from the towel and placed it in her spot on the dash. I stood there looking at it and the grief washed over me again like she had just died yesterday. I was a long way from the BVI and my boat was out of commission. I had managed to make a royal mess out of everything. *Way to go, Breeze.*

Just then, Howie came banging on the hull. "Wake up, ya boat bum," he growled. "We need to come to an agreement on fixing this old crate." I climbed down the ladder and said good morning. I asked about shore power. He showed me where I could plug in. When I reached for my wallet he shook me off. "You already give me a c-note. The repairs is gonna cost ya a pretty penny." We spent the next fifteen minutes looking under the hull. There were several large chunks of fiberglass missing. You could see the progression of whatever I had hit as it traveled down the hull until it slammed into the prop. The shaft was shot. The prop was mangled and the rudder had taken a hit as well. Howie assured me that this was a fixable for a price, but the real kicker was going to be the transmission. I didn't know squat about transmissions. "When ya stop an engine dead like that, it tears up everything," said Howie. These old Ford Lehmans might not be fast, but put out a lot of low-end torque."

"How much is a transmission?" Howie said he could order one rebuilt from American Diesel in Virginia for five grand or so, plus freight. It usually took a couple weeks. Installation would be another couple grand. The fiberglass work, new barrier, bottom paint, etc. would run seven or eight grand. He'd have to check on the prop and shaft, but figured another couple grand once it's all said and done. I was looking at fifteen grand, conservatively. Ouch.

"You got that kinda dough?" Howie put his hands on his hips and stared me right in the eyes. He had used his Jersey voice. It sounded like, "You talkin' to me?" I answered that yes, I had the money, but it would really hurt. He offered to piecemeal each job, finding the lowest bidder. The only problem was that it would take much longer that way. I really had no place to be. Without my boat I was stuck. I agreed to his terms and we shook hands. "You're going to be here for a while, Breeze. Remember, low profile."

This day wasn't starting out so good. I really needed a shower to clear my head.

I ended up showering in my own boat. I had installed a big poly water tank on the upper deck. When at anchor I'd just run a hose down and shower buck naked out on deck. I couldn't do that here. Instead I ran the hose through the port light in the head and showered right in the shower stall. I couldn't run the water pump due to the dead battery bank. After I got all cleaned up and shaved I set off on foot to find breakfast. Directly across from the city marina, I found a dumpy-looking little diner called the Stuffed Pig. From the outside it looked like a shithole, but I was hungry. A greeter directed me around back where I found a tropical oasis. My waitress reminded me of that lady from Mel's Diner. I kept waiting for her to say "kiss my grits," but she never did. I had a fantastic breakfast of lobster Benedict, with bacon and orange juice. That little feast set me back twenty bucks, with a five dollar tip to my TV diner waitress. This town was going to be expensive.

What to do, what to do? I wandered a bit on Highway 1. There really wasn't much to see except strip mall after strip mall. I found my way to the back of the city marina where some old dudes were playing dominos under a shade tree. There were bikes chained up everywhere, shopping carts, mopeds and motorcycles all lined up in the corner. I thought maybe I needed a bike. Then I remembered my dinghy. I had left Patches tied up in the pit back at the boatyard. I hustled on back only to find it gone. I looked up at the lift operator and shrugged my shoulders. He stuck his head around the corner and pointed at the abandoned marina next to Burdines. "We drug it around there this morning. Howie says to keep it over there until your boat is fixed."

I was relieved it hadn't been stolen. I doubted anyone would want it though. It had patches upon patches. I called it the least likely to be stolen look. I had to pump it up every time I got in it to go somewhere. The paint was all peeled off the outboard. I had replaced the cooling water discharge hose with the tube from a ballpoint pen. The pull cord handle was wound up in electrical tape. I had tried using rubberized paint over some leaky seams; it didn't work and it was ugly. It was not a very inviting target for thieves. It started on the third pull and I set off in the general direction of Dockside, not really knowing where I was going. It was kind of like a metaphor for my life. I was drifting and aimless.

I spent the next month being sucked in by the vortex that is Marathon. I became a local. I found every restaurant and bar within walking distance, but I always gravitated back to Dockside. I hung out talking to Miles and watching Carol serve drinks. He showed me how to dinghy to Sombrero Beach. I'd spend my days just laying in the sun and my nights drinking beer and listening to music at the bar. All the best singer-songwriters in Florida came to play at Dockside. I had my own designated bar stool where I'd sit and listen to Captain Josh, Jimi Pappas, Howard Livingston, Paul Roush, Steve Tolliver and his band, and a host of others.

One night when it was slow at the bar, Carol came over and asked me what my story was. "I've got no story, Carol," I answered. "I'm just an aimless drifter."

"Nah," she said. "You're running from something. Everybody that runs ends up in the Keys. Mostly here or Key West." She questioned me with her eyes, wanting to hear my secrets. There was something about those eyes, but I wasn't telling. I didn't think The Man would find me here, but for the first time I got antsy to move on. I'd have to talk to Howie about speeding things up.

Six weeks and twenty-six thousand dollars later, *Leap of Faith* was back in the water. They had found serious structural damage where the shaft passes through the hull. Hand-laid fiberglass repair of this sort was a tedious job, and expensive.

My cash reserves had taken a massive hit. I lost confidence in my ability to get the newly-repaired vessel all the way to the BVI with what I had left. I had been burning through money like I had an unlimited supply. Dinners and beers and twenty-dollar tips to Carol didn't help much either. I was at another crossroads. I hadn't done so well at the previous ones. Instead of leaving town right away, I took a mooring ball. I needed to figure out my next move.

I skipped going to Dockside for the next three nights. I sat in my boat talking to an urn full of ashes. I asked Laura to help me decide what to do. She wasn't answering. Maybe she was upset with me for flirting with Carol every night. I had not been unfaithful though. I still had no interest in actually being with another woman. I just didn't have it in my heart. Those were three very sad nights alone. I went through the photo albums again, fondly remembering our life together. I went back over our conversations about living on a boat in Paradise. Somehow I rationalized that we didn't really have the BVI as our goal. We talked about Florida, mostly, and Cayo Costa specifically. I could go back to Pelican Bay. Laura had been there once. We rented a boat out of Punta Gorda and

ED ROBINSON

spent the day on the beach. She was awed by the clear blue water and soft white sand. I wasn't sure about spreading her ashes there though. Maybe I'd just hang onto them for a while. Maybe someday I'd catch a break and have the resources to get her to BVI. The decision was made. I was taking *Miss Leap* and Laura to Pelican Bay.

Howie and Miles went out with me for a quick sea trial. Miles made some adjustments to the newly installed stuffing box and checked the shaft for alignment and vibration. Howie told Miles that he was "going to miss that old boat bum", meaning me. After we docked back at the marina, we agreed to meet for one final time at Dockside. I showered up and put on my nicest shirt. I was going to miss that place.

As I entered Carol came out from behind the bar and gave me a great big hug. It was a bit more than a friendly hug. She really wrapped me up and snuggled her nose against my neck. She whispered in my ear. "It was only going to take a few more nights to get me in your bed Breeze." I told her that if it wasn't for Miles, maybe I'd stick around for as long as it took. I didn't really mean it. It was a reflex left over from my old woman-chasing days. I hadn't had sex since before Laura died, and

I doubted I was ready for the likes of Carol. Maybe I'd never be ready for anyone.

Up on stage Eric Stone started strumming his guitar. This always got everyone's attention. He sang a song about his love for the sea that almost brought a tear to my eye. I was about to renew my relationship with the sea, after too long on the hard. When he finished he told the audience that "the song is for our good friend Breeze, who is leaving us tomorrow". This brought several of the regulars over to buy me drinks. I got too many Landsharks bought for me and then we started slamming shots of Lime Bite. The island songs played on. It was a fine final night. Other than Carol and Miles, I hadn't really made friends with the regulars. I just sat on my barstool alone every night and didn't mingle. They were always cordial though. If I wasn't such a broken-down mess, I would have made an effort to get to know them better. Most of them seemed like good solid folks. I promised myself that if I ever could, I'd return and do a better job, be a better friend. I really was going to miss this place.

Finally, I shoved off from the bar. I tried to hold Carol at arm's length to say goodbye. She was having none of it. She grabbed me by the collar and pulled me into her, planting a real nice kiss square on my lips. There was no tongue, but she held us together firmly for a few seconds before releasing me. There might have been a slight grinding against my hips. Breeze Junior started to stir. Then she shoved me away hard towards the door. "It's been nice to meet your acquaintance, Mr. Breeze." I tipped my cap and bowed slightly at the waist before spinning and walking slowly out the door. That girl was an enigma to me, a real damn puzzler.

As soon as I entered the salon on *Leap of Faith*, Laura's urn caught my eye. I immediately felt guilty, like I needed to apologize for getting hugged and kissed by Carol, and liking it. I spoke out loud. "I'm so sorry," I said to the urn. "Please forgive me."

RETURN TO CAYO COSTA

I LEFT BEFORE DAWN THE NEXT morning. It would be nine or ten hours to get back to Little Shark, twenty if I pushed on to Marco. I was undecided. I needed to see how the boat reacted. I really wanted to skip the Everglades and those damn mosquitoes, but I didn't want to push the boat, or myself, too hard the first day out. I ended up anchoring offshore, three miles shy of the Little Shark River. I hoped the mosquitoes wouldn't find me there.

I brought Laura out on the aft deck and we watched the sun set on the Gulf of Mexico. The soft rollers gently rocked us. I was conflicted in my feelings. It felt good to get out of the vortex of Marathon. It felt good to be moving again. I'd lost my paranoia about The Man finding me. On the other hand, I was heading north. I wasn't on my way to the BVI. I was quickly running out of money. I had failed at my mission, the one thing that had kept me going since Laura's death. If I didn't create some sort of income, not only would I never make the trip, I'd starve. I'd been living a life of luxury, eating and drinking my money down the drain. The boat repairs were a huge setback financially.

As I was mulling over my dismal-looking future, I watched the very last sliver of the sun wink out over the horizon. That's when I saw it. A split second of green flashed on the horizon where the sun used to be. I'd heard about the Green Flash, but I had never seen it. I believed it was real before; now I'd witnessed it with my own eyes. It sparked something in me. It seemed so magical. Ideas started careening around in my head. Ways to survive, and to make some cash, entered my mind. The heavens had given me some hope. *Maybe we'll make it after all, Laura.*

I had the same kind of traveling choice the next day. I really didn't like Marco Island much. Factory Bay was a muddy mess and there were few options ashore. It was ten hours north. If I pushed on to Fort Myers Beach, which I did like, it would be a sixteen-hour day at sea. The well-marked entrance channel to Matanzas Pass wouldn't be a problem in the dark. As I rounded the Cape Romano Shoals south of Marco, I decided to keep chugging north for Fort Myers Beach. The boat was humming along, the seas were calm. I had a long quiet day to think. I was beginning to formulate a plan. As crazy as it first sounded, I had talked myself into it. I was going to grow dope on the island of Cayo Costa. I could get a good crop growing before I ran out of money. I knew enough people in Punta Gorda to sell it to, some in volume. I never smoked the shit myself, but I didn't care if other people did. Live and let live.

I got in and grabbed a mooring ball late in the evening. It was too late to go into the Matanzas Inn and pay for it, but they ran a pretty loose operation there. I could pay in the morning, no problem. I was tired enough to resist the urge to go to the Upper Deck and drink beer. The last time I was there I heard John Friday play and he was pretty good. Another time I had listened to Scotty Bryan and had a lot of fun. As miserable as I was most of the time, music seemed to help my spirits and take my mind off my grief. Instead I put a Jim Morris CD in the laptop and listened to *Here Today, Fiji Tomorrow*, which was one of my favorites. It had been Laura's favorite too.

I spent all the next day walking backing and forth across the bridge, carrying big bags of potting soil and associated growing supplies. The next day I took the trolley to the Army/Navy store. I picked up an olive drab backpack, a folding shovel, and a camouflage poncho. I was going to be like Rambo, sneaking through the mangrove jungles to tend to my pot plants. I didn't know squat about growing pot, but the Green Flash had given me the inspiration.

The other inspiring idea I got that night was to make homemade rum. If I was going to be poor, I wouldn't be buying much rum from the liquor store. I spent my third day in Fort Myers Beach in the laundry room, pirating Wi-Fi. I researched how to make a still, and looked up rum recipes. On day four it was back to the hardware store for a great big stock pot and some copper tubing. I also picked up a small propane burner and assorted plumbing supplies to finish off the project. I lugged a twenty pound propane tank in the backpack across the bridge. It got heavier with every step. I must have been an odd sight crossing that bridge carrying a stockpot and copper tubing, while hunched over under the weight of the backpack.

I tried to cultivate a crazy-eyed look to finish off my ensemble.

If anyone was watching and questioning what the hell I was doing loading all this stuff on the boat, they didn't say anything. The boaters in Fort Myers Beach pretty much mind their own business. It's a good quality for a place to have, especially for a felon like myself. I had one last piece of business to take care of before I could leave. I needed pot seeds. I was pretty sure the guy on Bay Dreamer could help me out. He was recovering from cancer and smoked pot all day long. I had talked to him while he was anchored out near me in Punta Gorda. It was a stroke of luck that he was here now.

I scored big time. He had a strange habit of collecting his seeds. He kept them in old-time film canisters, a true child of the sixties. He had them in a rack like they were spices or something. Each was labeled with the name of its variety, like "Keys Gold", or "Purple Haze". Some just had the first name of the supplier on them, like "Bad Tom", or "Anna Banana". He schooled me on the particular qualities of each strain. I spent a couple hours with him. His name was Jamie Brown. At first glance he was just a dope-smoking boat bum. The more I talked with him, the more I respected his knowledge of not only dope, but sailing and living aboard. He was an old salt that I could learn from. He was no dummy either. Under the haze lay a hidden intelligence. I liked him. I hoped he kicked cancer's ass.

Finally, I was off. I was bound for my final destination on this trip. It was an easy five-hour cruise up the Intercoastal Waterway. I slid under the Sanibel Causeway and into San Carlos Bay. As we turned north Saint James City showed to starboard, Ding Darling to port. We motored into Pine Island Sound, past Captiva Island, by the Captiva Pass, past Cabbage Key and Useppa and finally we entered Pelican Bay on the north end of Cayo Costa. The entire area was rich with pirate history, so I abandoned my Rambo persona in favor of Gasparilla, the famed bloodthirsty pirate of local lore. Aarrgh! I was a dope-growing, rum-brewing, embezzling pirate.

I dropped anchor in the far southern end of the anchorage. I wanted to be as close to my target growing area as possible. There was a little cove off Murdoch Bayou with very little boat traffic. There was very little foot traffic on that part of the island too. It was uninhabited, overgrown and wild, and full of mosquitoes. Not a place you'd bump into tourists. My only concerns would be air traffic, which was fairly frequent, and park rangers. I intended the poncho to be a good cover to hide under whenever I heard a helicopter. The backpack would hide my supplies from casual observation as I ferried back and forth in the dinghy.

I spent the first few days just going to the beach and working on my tan. I beached the dinghy where I intended to when I started farming. I wanted to see if any people came around or crossed my path. The only ranger I saw was riding a four-wheeler on the beach. I was satisfied that this part of the island was isolated enough for my purposes. Operation Island Smile would soon commence. That's the brand name I chose for my dope. If anyone asked where it came from, I'd say "It came from the islands, mon."

I started germinating seeds the next day. The Eisenglass enclosure made a terrific greenhouse. Once they started to sprout I transferred them to trays. The plants that survived were then transplanted again into larger pots, the kind you buy tomato plants in. Lots of the seeds failed to germinate. Then I burnt the first good batch of sprouts up in the greenhouse. It was too hot for the tiny plants apparently. Two weeks into Operation

Island Smile and I had not one pot plant. *Geez, Breeze, you suck.* I threw another batch of seeds in to germinate. This time the ones that sprouted were brought down into the main cabin and kept in the shade until they grew stronger. Finally, I had a dozen good healthy plants to take to the island.

Each morning before dawn I'd take one plant, a bag of potting soil, and my folding shovel to a different spot on the island, well off any trails. I'd crawl around in the sea grapes looking for a clearing that was hidden from view. Then I'd dig out a hole in the sand and shell. I'd fill the hole with potting soil and transplant my little cash crops. A bottle of water was sprinkled around and the plant was left to fend for itself. Every few days I'd sneak back to them and give them some more water. If it rained a decent amount I'd let them be. I left subtle signs on the trail to mark my entry points. I needed to be able to find them all again. An odd rock, a stick stuck in the dirt, anything to clue me in. I got ten of the twelve plants to take hold and continue to grow. It was a start.

I set more seeds out to germinate and started working on my still. I explored a different island to scout out a likely spot to run a still and not be found. On Punta Blanca, I found a very secluded little clear spot well into the interior. The surrounding mangroves were twenty-feet tall. It didn't appear anyone ever walked through this spot. The walls of vegetation around the small clearing were unbroken and undisturbed. I had to literally low-crawl to get in. It would do nicely. I finished up construction of my little still and took it piece by piece into my new distillery. First I ran plain water through it. Then I had to make up a sacrificial batch of rum that would be thrown away. Only alcohol would sufficiently clean the byproducts of soldering out of the connections and render the future product potable. It was a sad thing pouring several gallons of freshly brewed rum on the ground that first time.

Finally I was ready to make my first batch of rum. I loaded the stock pot with water and molasses and fired it up. I sat with it for hours, adjusting the heat and watching the steam turn to liquid and slowly drip out the other end of the tubing into a spotless five-gallon bucket. I strung my poncho overhead of the whole rig to hide it from view from above. I swatted mosquitoes. Sweat ran down my face. It was boring. It was watching water boil. I had some vague romantic notion of old time bootleggers and rum runners in my head. This was nothing like that at all.

The five gallons of mash yielded half that much rum. The rum it made was over proof, which means it was really, really strong. It tested out at almost one-hundred-and-fifty proof. Adding two and half gallons of water diluted it to seventy-five proof, and gave me five gallons of finished product. I put a lid on the bucket and lugged my first batch of homegrown rum back to the boat. I had dumpster dived a bar in Fort Myers Beach to acquire a bunch of empty bottles. They didn't have caps on them, but I found a bunch of wine corks in that same dumpster that did the trick. Before I capped off each bottle, it got a shot of vanilla extract and a good squeeze of lime juice. I was trying to copy Lime Bite, my favorite rum. It had been Laura's favorite too. I poured a bit of melted wax over the corks and stowed them in the dark under my settee. It was tempting to have a taste, but I wanted to let it emulsify and age at least a little.

Meanwhile, the original pot plants were chest high and surviving. A new batch of seedlings was ready to transplant into bigger pots. Both of my enterprises were up and running nicely. I dubbed the rum Punta Blanca after the island of its birth.

I was keeping busy and not wallowing in the grief that had plagued me for so long. Laura was still on my mind all of the time, but having something to do eased the weight of her loss a little bit. Each evening I'd bring her out on the aft deck to watch the sun set over Cayo Costa. I would imagine her sitting next to me, holding my hand. I kept waiting to see the Green Flash again, but it did not show. The Green Flash had led me in this direction and I was grateful. I didn't know if it was going to be profitable, but it was giving me purpose. Growing dope and cooking up rum was easing my pain somehow. I forgot all about the BVI. I concentrated on my chores. I sat on the beach and watched the waves. I swam in the warm waters of the Gulf. I hiked the islands. I hadn't talked to another human in a month, but that was okay. Laura and I were doing just fine by ourselves.

SELLING DOPE AND RUM

I WAS CRAWLING THROUGH THE UNDERBRUSH to water my crop when I heard it coming. The distinctive sound of helicopter blades was getting louder. I pulled a branch out the way to sneak a peek. It was the mosquito-control chopper, spraying who knows what pesticide on the south end of the island. It was coming directly towards me. I quickly pulled my poncho out of the backpack and crouched down underneath it for protection. It passed over me and I waited for the spray to descend on me. The growth was so thick it never really made it. I could smell it though, and my eyes watered a bit. I needed some fresh air, but I didn't want to be seen by the chopper pilot. So far, no one had seen me coming and going, tending to my plants. Eventually he went back north and I crawled out from under and took a few good breaths. Close one.

Water was becoming a problem. I didn't have an unlimited supply. I caught rainwater when I could, but sometimes it didn't rain for several days. There used to be a spigot at the dinghy dock near the ranger station, but they took it out. Then they took out the whole damn dinghy dock. The park service docks still remained, and I used them to sneak up to the restrooms and fill a five gallon jug with water after dark.

Brewing up a batch of rum used a lot of water. It took seven or eight gallons of water to produce five gallons of rum. Then I needed to clean the still afterwards. Speaking of the rum, I taste tested the first batch at one month in. The first sensation was a pretty nasty bite, but it left a pleasant aftertaste. It had a raw alcohol quality to it that I wasn't sure people would like. I hoped that after a little more aging it would mellow. I also decided to add a little less vanilla and a little more lime to the next batch. After two months, the original batch was much better, pretty damn good actually, except for the excess vanilla taste. It tasted a lot like regular Captain Morgan. A couple of months later the second batch came out close to perfect. There was just the right amount of lime in the aftertaste, and no nasty bite going down.

Some of the pot plants looked ready to harvest. If I let them get too tall they'd be seen eventually. I didn't know if you could cut a part of the plant and the rest would continue to grow, or if you were supposed to just cut the whole thing down. I did a test. I chopped half of one plant down and stuffed it in a trash bag, and then into the backpack. I hung it up to dry in my enclosure. With all the plastic zipped up it got quite hot inside during the day. A few days later I checked the part of the plant I had left and it was noticeably withering. I chopped down the rest and hung it up to dry too. Soon I had several pounds of market-ready dope. I hoped my old acquaintances in Punta Gorda would be willing to deal.

I needed a discreet place to dock, so I put in a call to Big Lloyd. He said his own boat was at his dock, but the dock at the vacant lot next door was open. He'd call the owner and ask permission. He called back with a proposition. If I'd cut the grass I could use it. I could use his mower. The last thing I wanted to do was cut grass. I'd been cutting my own kind of grass for the past few weeks. I didn't want to anchor out in the open, though, so I accepted. When I arrived, Big Lloyd was there to grab my lines, which was helpful. *Miss Leap* is a single screw vessel with no bow thruster and not very nimble around docks. We shook hands and he said he had another proposition. If I would cut his grass, and generally look out after his place when he was gone, I could use this dock whenever I wanted. I told him I'd think it over. No way could I stay in one place too long, at least not in town where I could be found.

I started making phone calls to old friends that I knew or suspected smoked dope. You wouldn't believe how many strait-laced, middle-class, law-abiding citizens smoke the stuff. Good people living good lives, not bothering anyone is how I saw it. First I called Anna, and she called Effie and Bryan. Word got around the old circle pretty quick. I had lucked out. A certain supply route had dried up and the locals were jonesing. Anna called back and said she had five friends ready to buy. My big target was AA Art. I had hung out with him in the local bars. Art didn't drink. In fact, he was an avid member of Alcoholics Anonymous. Art smoked pot, had for forty years. He also sold a little on the side. He asked if I had a pound. Score!

Over the next few days I met all the buyers in assorted meeting places around town and sold all that I had. I still had several mature plants on the island and new seedlings underway. It looked as if Operation Island Smile was going to be profitable after all.

I turned my attention to getting rid of the rum. First stop was Fisherman's Village to see my buddies Colorado Bob and Kentucky Tom. We all sat under the gazebo and tasted my product. I used the second, better batch. Both agreed that it was pretty decent. I couldn't be more proud of myself. Sitting in the mangroves swatting mosquitoes in the Florida heat watching water boil is no fun chore. Dodging DDT sprayed from a helicopter wasn't much fun either, come to think of it. I offered a special deal, just for my closest friends, at ten dollars per bottle. Bob took three and Tom took two, saying he was short on cash. Tom was always short on cash.

After a few hours catching up with the boys, I shoved off in the dinghy for Gilchrest Park. I found Cross-Eyed John sitting in the shade of a pavilion. I gave him a taste of the first batch and his eyes grew wide. I thought he was going to spit it out, but then he smiled. I offered him the same deal, ten dollars per bottle. He rounded up the rest of the bums and together they had fifty bucks between them. Five more bottles sold. I wasn't going to get rich with the Operation Punta Blanca, but I managed to cultivate a few customers on this trip. There was a bum party in Gilchrest Park that night.

Back at Big Lloyd's I filled my water tanks and jerry jugs from his garden hose. After picking up some supplies in town I was ready to shove off. He came out to ask me about his proposition. I thanked him for the offer but had to turn it down. I'm pretty sure he was disappointed, but I knew it would eventually lead to trouble of some sort. I never was sure if he was being sincerely kind, or if he just needed a caretaker. Under different circumstances we could have been friends, but I was resigned to my life on the lam. It was time to get back to Pelican Bay and get back to work.

After stopping off in Burnt Store Marina for diesel fuel, I cruised down Charlotte Harbor towards the Boca Grande Pass on a glass-calm day. I was feeling self-satisfied. I had made some money by my wits and wiles. It could be done. Then I started doing the math. The fuel was eight-hundred bucks. Food and provisions another two hundred. Various and sundry items for rum brewing and pot growing were another hundred. I came out ahead, but at this rate I calculated I could leave for the BVI in about four thousand years. *Great plan Breeze.*

That trip to town to peddle my wares turned out to be the best one I would ever have. Anna's gang had their supply route reopen. He was always available, not just coming to town once a month. AA Art continued to be a buyer, but in smaller quantities. Colorado Bob sailed off to the Caribbean for six months. Kentucky Tom was still good for two or three bottles, when he had the cash. Cross-Eyed John wanted to straighten out his life so he went on the wagon. The rest of the bums were unreliable. The last time I approached them they decided to gang up on me and just take the rum for free. Eventually they were rousted out by the police. If I had to buy fuel, I'd sometimes lose money on these trips. When I could skip the fuel dock, I have enough to buy a little food with very little left over.

Dinty Moore became my personal chef. I'd have canned chicken and dumplings one night, canned beef stew the next. When I got sick of that I'd catch a fish for dinner. I lost a ton of weight. I watched my money like a miser. I still had a small reserve for emergencies, but if I dipped into that I knew it would run out.

I kept planting more plants and cooking more rum hoping business would pick up. I talked Anna into taking an ounce every month whether she needed it or not. I think she agreed out of pity. I got Tom to talk some of his dock neighbors into taking a bottle or two. I was barely surviving. The BVI was a million miles away. I gave up hope on that dream. *I'm so sorry, Laura*. I started drinking the rum I couldn't sell. I tucked five bottles of my finest Punta Blanca away in the bilge for long-term aging and never touched them. Someday I'd have a reason to celebrate, at least that's what I told myself. I cursed the Green Flash. Then I cursed myself for believing that the Green Flash inspired the life I was living. *Stupid Breeze. Stupid Green Flash*.

ON THE RUN

ALL I HAD LEFT WAS my freedom, and I almost lost that one night on the C-Dock with Tom and Bob. When I ran from that agent, I decided to keep on running. I buried my still deep in the mangroves of Punta Blanca Island where no one would ever find it. I cut down most of the pot plants on Cayo Costa and hung them up to dry all at once. I left a few standing. If they made it, they made it. I had small hopes that if I ever returned, they would be there for me to harvest.

Once my work was done I took *Miss Leap* way out into the Gulf and steered a course for the Dry Tortugas. The Man would never find me there. After twenty-seven hours of trying to stay awake, I finally dropped anchor off Fort Jefferson on Garden Key. Again I wished for an autopilot. I spent two weeks fishing and exploring. Most of the time, I was the only boat in the harbor. I traded some fishermen a case of hot beer for a five-gallon bucket full of shrimp. Good thing I like shrimp, because I ate them for a week. It was a nice break from my Dinty Moore diet.

I couldn't stay here forever. The Tortugas are called dry for a reason. There is no fresh water. The closest civilization, if you can call it that, is Key West. I had reservations about stopping at the world's biggest non-stop party, but I thought I could probably sell some dope there.

I dropped anchor next to Fleming Island just in time for happy hour. I nursed one beer each in several bars before I identified a likely suspect. By some bizarre coincidence, the guy tells me his name is Bad Tom. It couldn't be. "Do you know a guy named Jamie Brown on Bay Dreamer?" I asked. "Sure do", was the reply. "Me and Jamie are buds."After explaining how I met Jamie I got down to business. Bad Tom assured me he could help sell some Island Smile. He bought an ounce on the spot and said it would be a day or two but he'd get back to me. I told him the name of my boat so he could find me in the anchorage. I promptly blew most of my newly-acquired money on Duvall Street. Key West is expensive after happy hour. It's also the place where hundreds, if not thousands of fugitives come to hide. If I was a G-man, I'd just sit on Duvall and wait for my mark to walk by.

Bad Tom managed to find me two buyers and I used that money to restock the pantry and take on fuel again. I was still broke. I went back west and hid out near Boca Grande Key until my food stores got low again. When I returned to Key West I learned that Bad Tom had sailed to the Dominican, lost his boat on a reef and broken his hip. I tried with no success to meet someone else to sell dope to, but I didn't want to spend too much money in the bars. The dinghy dock was a bust. I looked like a beggar hanging around in my tattered clothes. I couldn't take a chance on getting arrested either. A pot possession charge would be the least of my worries.

I walked Duval aimlessly until some music caught my ear. I was outside Willy T's when I heard it. The sign said happy hour beers were two bucks. What the heck. I took a stool and listened to a guy named Captain Josh sing about parrotheads in paradise. He was different, a nice break from the usual Key West fare. I blew ten bucks. Each time I finished a beer, he'd start another song that made me stay for another. I had to get out of this town.

I decided I better make my exit from Key West. Marathon, (and Dorado's Dockside) was just eight hours up the Keys. I was down to eating out of cans again, and I didn't have many cans left. I started splitting each serving into two, and ate only once per day. I was skin and bones, with a deep tan from my days on the islands. The wrinkles around my eyes were sharper. The veins in my arms stood out prominently. I didn't like what I saw in the mirror. I had always been a good-looking guy. There was no lying to myself about how bad I looked now. If I didn't catch a break in Marathon, I'd be nearing the end of the line. Maybe Howie or Eric Stone would let me work off the books, for cash.

I couldn't afford a marina, or even a mooring ball, so I had to anchor in the mud just inside the bridge. It was where the undesirables lived. At low tide *Miss Leap* would be sitting on the bottom, but I had no other option. It was also a long dinghy ride from the Dockside, which I took after cleaning up as best I could. My best-looking shirt hung off me like it was two sizes too big. My best remaining pair of shorts had a few holes in them. My flip flops had been repaired with gorilla glue and a bread tie.

As soon as I walked in, Carol practically screamed, "Breeze!" She ran out from behind the bar to give me a hug. She stopped just short and took a closer look at me. I did the same to her. "You look like shit Mr. Breeze," she said. "Nice to see you too, Carol." She apologized and sat me at the bar and told me to tell her all about it. She brought me a cold Landshark. I couldn't help but notice she had put on a few pounds. She also had dark circles under her eyes. Those eyes that once entranced me had lost some of their sparkle. I could have told her that she looked like shit too, but I kept my mouth shut.

"What can I get you sailor?" she asked.

"Shit, Carol, I can't afford anything in here. I can't even afford this beer."

"That bad huh? Well don't you worry tonight. I'll bring you a burger and some fries. Beers are on me."

I thought back on all those twenty-dollar tips I had left for her.

I was grateful for her kindness and told her so. She winked and said she'd get paid back, one way or another. There she goes again. That was definitely flirtatious. Where was Miles?

For the rest of the night, every time she passed by she would touch me, or make a sexual innuendo of some sort. There was no attempt to hide it. It was pretty blatant. Miles was nowhere in sight. Even though she had let herself go a little, she was still an attractive woman, but I had no intentions of getting involved with her. I had multiple reasons. She was married, of course, but even if she wasn't, I was in no way mentally or emotionally prepared for any sort of tryst. I spent my days mourning the loss of my wife. I couldn't spend my nights chasing other women. Finally, I was a wreck. I was an underfed, sun-baked, dope peddler who brewed homemade rum in his spare time. I talked to an urn full of ashes. I was also an embezzler and tax evader attempting to keep a low profile.

I started wondering why I had returned to the vortex in Boot Key Harbor. I wondered how I was ever going to leave. Other than my emergency stash, I was busted. I had a brief thought of selling *Miss Leap*, but dismissed it immediately. Without the boat, I'd be no better than the bums in Gilchrest Park. She needed fuel, and I needed food. *Sell the dope, Breeze*.

I got off my barstool and milled about in the crowd until I recognized one of the locals. Tiki

Terry was well-connected in this town. He had his own bar in his backyard that I had visited once to see Jimmy Parrish play. I didn't know if he smoked dope, but there was a good bet he knew who did. He was also good friends with Miles. He remembered me and gave me a good firm handshake and a friendly hello. I thought to myself, here's one of those people I should have gotten to know better. I didn't want to just jump right in and ask him to buy some dope, so I started a little small talk.

"You seen Miles around?" I asked.

"You didn't know? Miles took off a few months ago. Carol has been a mess since."

I was in disbelief. They had seemed like such a happy couple. Terry explained that Miles decided he wanted to sail to the Bahamas. Carol wanted no parts of it. When they made the trip to Marathon they had a bad crossing of Florida Bay. It scared her so bad she was done with sailing. She'd live on the boat in a nice, safe, protected harbor like Boot Key, but she'd be damned if she was going offshore again. They had a huge fight about it one night, and Carol left to stay with a friend. The next morning Miles and *Crew Zen*, were gone.

"I see her over there coming on to you Breeze," said Terry. "You gonna hit that?"

"Nah man, I got too many problems of my own. You might be able to help me with one of them."

He said, "What can I do for you?"

"I need to get rid of some smoking dope Terry. You know anyone? I'm kinda desperate."

"You've come to the right place my man," he chuckled. "I know everyone in this bar that smokes. Toke a little myself occasionally."

He motioned me outside and we talked things over. He offered to host a party for the gang and smooth the way for me with my potential customers. He was always throwing great parties. I should have gone to more of them. We ironed out the details and I returned to my stool. I had a glimmer of hope, at least for the short term.

Carol walked up behind me and put both hands on my ass and gave my cheeks a squeeze. She said, "We need to put some meat on those bones, honey. You sure you have the strength to go a few rounds in your bunk with me?"

"I heard about Miles," I replied. "I'm real sorry."

"Miles ain't here, and you are. Scratch my back and I'll scratch yours, or anything else you need scratching."

I liked her. I didn't want to hurt her feelings, especially after the free meal and beers. "I can't Carol," I said. "I'm real sorry, but I just can't."

"You can't get it up?" she asked. "A virile looking man like you?"

"No, that's not it," I replied. "It worked the last time I checked. I've got other problems Carol. Problems you don't need to hear about."

"I'm all ears when you're ready, Breeze."

There was no chance of that ever happening.

I changed the subject by excusing myself and thanking her for the generosity. I promised to pay her back soon and made my escape. I thought maybe I ought to stay away from Dockside, but it was the only real redeeming quality of this town. I was fond of Carol; I just didn't want to screw her, or anyone else.

I sat on the boat and wondered if I'd ever have sex again. I doubted that I would ever make real love to another woman, but maybe someday I could just fuck someone. Someday was far, far in the future, maybe never.

Tiki Terry's party was a huge success. He had privately told each attendee that I was there with the good stuff, and that I really needed the money. It was like a charity event and I should have been ashamed. Beggars can't be choosers though, so I made deal after deal. I emptied the backpack of dope and filled it with cash. Carol was working at Dockside so I could relax for the night. I fell all over myself thanking Terry afterwards.

I boarded *Miss Leap* and headed straight for my bunk. Carol was laying there naked. She propped up on one elbow and used one finger to give me the come hither motion. I just stood there. I got a good look at her body and I was truly tempted. The light was just right to hide the flaws and accentuate the good parts. I was feeling sporty after my success at the party. I was buzzed but not too drunk. Then I spotted Laura's urn. Any visions of letting myself go with Carol quickly evaporated. It wasn't going to happen.

"Damn it, Breeze," she yelled at me. "You know you want to. What the hell?"

"I wish I did want to, Carol," I said, looking down at the floor. "If I could bring myself to do it, I'd do it with you."

"Tell me, Breeze. What's got you all broken up inside?"

I turned and walked out. I sat on the aft deck with my head in my hands. I held back tears. *Breeze, Breeze, Breeze, how did you ever get so fucked up?*

She came out in one my shirts and took the other deck chair. We sat in silence for a long time. It's rare for two people to sit quietly for long without feeling uncomfortable, but there we sat. We looked over at each other a few times. She gave me a nice smile and touched the back of my hand.

"I hope you conquer your demons someday, Breeze." It was nice. It sounded sincere. I didn't want to think about my demons anymore today though.

"Go to Miles," I said. "Track him down. Fly over there and join him. You two belong together."

We sat in more silence. Finally she rose and started for the kayak that I didn't notice when I returned to the boat.

"Not that I should take advice from someone as messed up as you," she said. "But I'm going to try to find Miles. You're right. It's my fault for not sharing his dream."

She got me to chuckle at that one, and the tension eased. I helped her board the kayak and untied her from Miss Leap. As she started to paddle away she hollered back over her shoulder. "If this shit don't work out, I'm tracking you down Breeze."

I shouted back across the water. "Good luck finding me, missy. That's why they call me the Breeze."

I heard her laughing as she disappeared into the darkness. It was the last time I ever saw her. I hope she found her man.

STAYING ON THE MOVE

CALLED TERRY TO THANK HIM for hooking me up with the pot-buying party. The man practically saved my life. I'd never done a thing for him. Yup, most certainly someone I should have been a better friend to.

He asked, "So what, did you find a bale floating off the coast or something?"

"Yea, something like that," I answered. "Hey, I might be able to come across some more. If so, can I come see you?"

"You're welcome here anytime Breeze," he said. "Lots of dope goes through this town."

My thoughts were on those plants I left growing back on Cayo Costa. I had money for fuel and nothing else but time. I decided to island hop a bit, then head north again to familiar waters. As I pulled up to the fuel dock at the boatyard,

Howie was standing next to the pumps with his arms crossed. He looked annoyed.

"I'm disappointed in you, Breeze," he scowled as he grabbed my lines. "First you don't stop by to say hello. Then after all that work we did on this old tub's running gear, you park it over there in the mud with the derelicts."

"I had no choice at the time," I said. "But things are looking up now. Fill her up please."

He raised an eyebrow at that, knowing how high the tab was going to be. Two hundred gallons and a thousand bucks later, I backed off the dock with a hearty wave to Howie.

"Robbery on the high seas, I tell ya," I hollered across the fairway. "I'm never coming back to this den of thieves."

I got the one-finger salute from Howie as he turned and walked back up the gangway.

First stop was to be Islamorada. I planned to take the inside route, on the Florida Bay side. It's full of tricky shallows but I had a secret weapon. A former dock neighbor, Business Bob, had merged his chart plotters waypoints and routes with mine. This would be the first time I'd get to put it to good use. I couldn't believe his generosity and willingness to help at the time. I thought it would be a great aid in navigating down through the Bahamas on my way to BVI. As I punched up his preplanned route to Islamorada, I thought that he was another person who I could have been a better friend to. *You suck, Breeze.*

The trip up was uneventful. Miss Leap purred the whole way. I managed not to run aground, and I found a decent spot to anchor right out in front of the Lorelei. I spent a few days visiting the highlights of the area. I spent a couple hours at Worldwide Sportsman. I made a side trip to Bud and Mary's Fish Camp. I spent a day out at Shell Key. I took a walk through Lignumvitae State Park, which I cut short due to the ferocity of the mosquitoes.

I sipped one margarita each evening at the Lorelei and watched the sun go down. Bringing Laura out on the aft deck with me every night was starting to creep me out. I knew it was bizarre behavior, but if I was on the boat at sundown I'd still do it. I still talked to her sometimes. I talked to *Miss Leap* too. They were the only two things I felt close too. *You're a strange bird Breeze.*

I moved up into Blackwater Sound off Key Largo for a few days. I found a bar called Coconuts that would have been fun if I was one to have fun.

Finally I'd had enough. The pot plants on Cayo Costa were calling me. Another score like the last one and I would have enough money to last for many months. Maybe I could make this a regular thing. Grow the plants, ship them back down to Marathon, and really start making money. I had plenty of seeds remaining, plus each new harvest yielded more seeds. Make a dozen trips or so, save up and start thinking about the BVI again.

I pointed *Leap of Faith* northwest towards Flamingo, rounded Cape Sable and turned north for the Boca Grande Pass. I skipped Little Shark, Marco, and even Fort Myers Beach. We chugged along at our stately six knots all the way to Cayo Costa and Pelican Bay. I was tired, but it felt good to be home. I slept for twelve hours straight and awoke to the brilliant Florida sunshine beaming in through the port lights. Dolphins circled on the hunt for breakfast. Ospreys chirped from the island.

I sat sipping coffee, contemplating my lot in life. I once ran a multi-million dollar company. Now I was about to crawl through the mangroves in hopes that some neglected pot plants had survived on their own. The way things had gone wrong for me, odds were the rangers had found them, chopped them down and were staking out the place right now. I decided to clean up and play tourist, case the island first.

I looked myself over in the mirror. I had put some of the weight back on, which smoothed the wrinkles in my face. I had lost a bit of my tan, but I was still pleasantly brown. I had run out of rum long ago. As a result, my eyes were now clear. Chicks used to dig my deep blue eyes. I kept them hidden under dark sunglasses these days.

I took a beach chair, towel and small cooler with me. I landed the dinghy in the familiar cove I used so many times. Walking across the island I looked casually around for any signs of activity. I passed by a few of my discreet markers and they appeared undisturbed. I left the plants alone that day. Instead I just sat on the beach and read a book. *Black Palmetto* by Paul Carr held my interest pretty well. I lost myself in his Keys detective thriller all afternoon. I had been to some of the places in the book just recently. I decided he was a good writer and I'd try to find his other books if I could. I had picked that one up in the book exchange at the Marathon City Marina one day.

Originally I had planned to keep the same routine for a few more days, but the suspense was killing me. Very early the next day I went in search of survivors. I found them. They stood tall and bushy, full of buds. A few had peeked out above the mangroves and brush, but apparently no one had noticed them. I cut half of the tallest one down and stuffed it into my backpack. I hurried off the island to get my stash back to the boat. I was really paranoid that someone would figure out what I was doing.

I decided to return to my tourist routine. I spent the next day sitting on the beach reading *Ocean Floors*, by Rodney Riesel. His character was running all around the Keys too. Apparently I had developed an affinity for fiction set in the Keys. I thought my story would make a good book someday.

After two more days nonchalantly strolling back and forth across the island, I decided the coast was clear. I started cutting and drying, hauling pot in my backpack as fast as I could. I kept it to one trip per day so as not to arouse suspicion. I saw no one. No one saw me. When the harvest was finished, I began replanting. Germination, seedlings, transplants then transplants to the island kept me busy for a few weeks. I watered them consistently until I felt certain they had taken hold and would continue to grow.

I started eating better, or at least more. The occasional inspections in the mirror satisfied me that I was looking much better. I cut my hair and shaved one day, and thought I saw a glimpse of the old Breeze in my reflection. That evening I brought Laura out on deck to watch the sunset. I asked her a question. "What do you think Laura? Is this it for us, or will I ever move on?" She didn't answer. I had no answer either.

I shrugged and put the urn back on the dash. I needed to make preparations to return to Boot Key and peddle my dope. I should call Terry ahead of time, but I had no cell service here. I made the boat ready for a short hop down to Fort Myers Beach. I splurged when I got into Matanzas Pass. I took a mooring ball. For fifteen bucks per night I could take long hot showers, get rid of my trash, and take on water for my tanks. I'd call Terry in the morning.

I got all cleaned up, put on my best shirt, and took a good hard look in the mirror. I pronounced myself acceptable to the world. Not quite the stud I used to be, but not too bad either. I felt something different in the air, a hopeful anticipation. It took me a while to figure out what it was. I'd had no hope for so long now. I set off from the dinghy dock towards town with just a little spring in my step. I wanted a beer and to be near some other humans.

I chose the Smoking Oyster Brewery, mostly because it the first bar you come to on the main drag. It was well off the beach and catered more to locals than to tourists. The bar itself was full, but a few small tables sat empty. I moved towards the back corner to find one in the shade. That's when I saw her.

A MOST UNLIKELY REUNION

AT THE VERY BACK TABLE sat my long-lost college girlfriend. I hadn't seen her in over twenty-five years. I was certain that I'd never see her again. I'd thought about her often over the years, wondering how her life turned out. I stopped dead in my tracks. It was like seeing a ghost, a drop-dead gorgeous ghost from far in my past.

She said one word, "Meade?" No one has called me that since, well, since she did back in college.

I said, "Andi? I've been called Breeze for almost thirty years, but that's okay. I can't believe it's really you."

"I've been going by Andrea for that long too," she said, rising from her chair to greet me. "I'm as surprised as you are."

Andrea Mae Mongeon was my best friend and lover for the two years I lasted at Frostburg State College, in Western Maryland. She was a brilliant scholar. Her intellect amazed me. She was well versed on just about any topic from philosophy to politics to sports. She was way more sophisticated than I. She had attended the finest Catholic school in the suburban Washington D. C. area and graduated at the top of her class.

More importantly to a college freshmen, she was stunningly pretty. No movie actress or supermodel could match her natural beauty. She could have been a model or an actress, except for one thing. She stood five feet tall on her tiptoes. She weighed ninety-five pounds. She was a goddess in miniature. Her long straight hair was a dark brown, almost black. It shone like a shampoo commercial. Her brown eyes were flecked with gold, giving them a perpetual sparkle. She was blessed with a perfect nose, cheeks and chin. Her figure was equally perfect. She was perfectly proportioned for her small build. She had curves in just the right places, no extra fat anywhere, but still soft.

We had met on my second day at school. I was standing in line to register for classes. I was discussing with another guy how lame last night's college-sponsored social was. They put two dorms together and laid out punch and cookies, straight out of the fifties. This feminine voice from behind me said, "You were just at the wrong dorm. We had a great party at our place." I turned around and saw Andi for the first time. Let me tell you, I almost peed my pants. I had dated the best-looking girls at my high school, but in front of me stood a magnificent angel of the likes I had never seen before. She practically had an glow around her.

I managed not to stutter as I stuck out my hand in introduction. "My name is Meade Breeze," I said. "It's a pleasure to meet you. And your name is?"

"I'm Andrea Mongeon," she replied. "But my friends call me Andi."

"Great, my friends call me Breeze."

"Do you have a lot of friends, Mr. Breeze?" she asked.

I said, "Tons, but none as pretty as you."

That lame-ass line seemed to work. She gave me a coy smile and tucked her chin into her shoulder, curling a finger in her hair. I asked her out that very instant. She accepted. We spent the rest of that school year making love and expanding our minds, in more ways than one. She had an adventurous streak and actively sought out new experiences, in bed and out. Just being in her presence made me high. This was the period in my life when I started making a habit of thanking the Big Man Above for my blessings.

I was a pretty sharp guy, but it was apparent that she was smarter than me. I was a pretty good-looking guy, but I was an ugly mug compared to her. I was secretly intimidated by her. Good-looking, smart, nineteen-year-old baseball stars generally aren't intimidated by anything. So far in my young life I had had no fear, but with her I was different. I was in a perpetual state of disbelief that she was with me.

When the semester ended, we all relocated to Ocean City, Maryland for the summer. She shared a small apartment with five other hotties. I was in heaven. I ran the roads back and forth from my hometown to play ball. I'd bring some buddies down to give them a shot at Andi's girlfriends. She was waiting tables at Phillip's and would give me gas money. It was all like a dream.

During our second year of school we fell even more deeply in love. We discussed running away together to marry. Her father didn't like that one bit. His precious daughter had a guaranteed future. She wouldn't waste it on some dirt farmer who would never amount to anything. One night I sat her down and told her that the old man had a point. He was paying for her education. She had a free ticket to the good life. Marrying young and losing all that was irresponsible. She cried her eyes out that night. I thought I was being mature about the whole thing, which wasn't my strong point. Instead I had broken her heart. That was the last thing I had intended. I was so in love with her that it hurt. I ached all day long just thinking about her.

We stayed together and things returned to normal, but her father hatched a plan. He managed to arrange for her admittance into some fancy school in Europe. We had one last summer together. I quit school and enlisted in the Army. I'd ship out soon after her new school term began. Our love never ceased, but circumstances wrenched us apart.

We spoke on the phone many times. We sent each other long love letters. She got her degree, then continued on to get her Masters. She was in Germany for the fall of the Berlin Wall. I was sitting in a bar in San Antonio watching it on television.

By the time she returned to the States, I was in Houston working for a newspaper. By the time I returned to my hometown, I had a daughter. What I did not have was a wife. Andi had not married either. I took my little girl to visit her near D.C. We spent a day at the zoo and stayed the night at her place. She let me in her bed, but we just lay there and held each other. It was sweet. Our lives had taken paths that no longer intersected. She was going to work for NASA, and would make six figures. I was working for the local paper and bringing down two-hundred bucks a week. I reluctantly let go. When I said goodbye one final time, I knew it would be the last.

She was the one that got away. Wherever I was in my life from then on, I'd wonder about her. I'd remember her fondly. Sometimes it made me smile and sometimes it made me sad. I had a dozen relationships that didn't work out. Hell, getting women was easy for me. Keeping them was the hard part.

Laura changed all that. She was so perfect for me, that Andi was driven from my thoughts. Laura was beautiful too, just in different ways. She was smart too, not in Andi's academic way, but in a down-to-earth common sense way. Some men never meet a woman that is truly special. I had been blessed with two of them. I lost Laura a few years ago. She was gone and was never coming back. I had lost Andi decades ago. Now she was standing right in front of me.

She was every bit as magnificent as I remembered her. She was wearing a sheer sun dress and tiny little sandals. Breeze Junior took notice. I felt just like that nineteen-year old baseball player. She couldn't have gained more than five pounds since college. Her hair still shone. The gold flecks in her eyes were still sparkling. She tucked her chin into her shoulder, twirled her hair around one finger and said, "I'm so happy to see you, Meade, uh, or Breeze." Her coy smile was exactly as it had been on the first day we met.

"I'm incredibly happy to see you," I said. "A bit dumbfounded, but ecstatic otherwise. Can we sit and talk? Are you free?"

"I am free for you," she said. "Meade Edwin Breeze, in the flesh. I can't believe it."

"Of all of the gin joints in all of the world," I said, in my best Bogart voice. She laughed and said she wanted to hear all about my life. That popped my bubble a bit. What would I tell her? Instead I said I wanted to hear all about her life, which I was sure was much more interesting.

We talked for an hour, piling up the empty beer bottles. When I told her that I lived on a boat full-time and traveled the coast and the Keys, she got really excited.

"That's so cool, can I see the boat? Is it here?"

I thought maybe she wasn't the type to climb around docks and ride in dinghies and shower with a garden hose on the back deck. Getting her back to the boat though, seemed like a fantastic idea. I stood and extended my hand to help her up. "Your chariot awaits fair lady." She took my hand and we left the bar arm in arm. It felt as if no time had passed between us. Old lovers reunited.

On the way I explained that the boat was on a mooring ball out in Matanzas Pass. We'd take the dinghy out to it. She thought that sounded like fun. If was after dark now, and what I saw on the dock looked like no fun at all. Two shady characters blocked our path. Latinos: one small and wiry, the other taller and stocky; they didn't look like boaters to me. The little one was wearing slacks and black dress shoes. His button-down shirt had only the top button fastened, exposing lots of ink across his torso. I mentally named him Knife, because I figured he had one on his person somewhere. The bigger one I named Butch. He sported a crew cut. I figured I could take the little one if he didn't have a knife, but Butch looked strong and tough.

I hadn't been in a fight in twenty-five years, and I lost that one. The situation didn't look so good. *Breeze, you have a special kind of luck.*

One minute you're basking in the glow of the world's most beautiful woman, who was once your lover. The next moment you get to show her how much of a coward you are. I was trying to think quickly. How do I get us out of this?

"We just want her purse, mister," said Knife. He turned to her and held out his hand. "Don't do nothing stupid."

Just then, all one hundred pounds of pretty girl simply shoved him square in the chest, hard. It was the last thing he expected. His slippery street shoes came out from under him and overboard he went. While I'm standing there trying to think of something, she took action on her own. I saw her stomping Knife's fingers as he tried to grab on to the dock. I turned to face Butch. Her simple approach seemed to work so I was inspired to try to kick him in the balls. One flip flop went flying into the water, but I scored a middling hit with my bare foot. It was enough. He put his hands down to his crotch and bent over at the waist. I punted him in the chin with the same bare foot. He almost kept his balance, but as he teetered I gave him a shove and he joined his buddy in the drink.

Knife had lost purchase on the pier and the current was swiftly taking him north under the bridge. If he couldn't swim or grab on to something, he'd end up in the Gulf. Butch had managed to grasp a concrete pillar supporting the bridge. He was hugging it with all his might, but fear shone in his face. I doubted he could hold on for very long.

I hopped down the dock towards Andi. That second barefoot kick had struck hard bone and my foot hurt like hell.

"C'mon, let's get in the dinghy and haul ass," I advised.

"Aren't you going to call the police?" she asked.

"I can't. I really, really can't," I said. "That's the last thing I want to do. I'll explain later."

"Let me call them," she offered. "We can't just let them drown."

I didn't care if they drowned or got eaten by sharks, but I compromised with her.

"Okay, you call. Don't tell them who you are, or who I am, or what boat we are going to. It's important, Andi. I promise. I'll explain."

She dialed 911 to report two men in the water in the vicinity of the bridge over Matanzas Pass. She hung up as soon as they started asking questions.

"It always was exciting being with you," she said, "Maybe too exciting."

We boarded the dinghy and set out for the big boat. She still had her purse. I was short one flip flop.

I assured her that my life was anything but exciting these days. We rode the dinghy through all the moored boats to the back of the mooring field where *Miss Leap* sat waiting. On the way I mulled over how much I would divulge. I was still feeling the adrenaline from our encounter on the dinghy dock. I was also still trying to come to terms with running into Andi here. I didn't think about Laura, or the urn prominently displayed on the dash.

I gave her a quick tour of the boat and she seemed impressed. In spite of its age, it really was a nice boat. She asked purposeful questions about life aboard, and my travels. When the tour was complete, she went to the urn.

"I don't know, Breeze. It all seems very romantic and carefree, but I sense there is more to it than that. Is it also sad and lonely?"

I looked down at the floor and considered my reply.

"Yes, Andi," I said, almost under my breath. "It's more sad and lonely than you can imagine. I doubt you want to hear how sad it's been."

She approached me, extending her hand and touching my cheek very softly.

"I want to hear all about it," she whispered. "It's been a long time Breeze. Tell me what's happened to you."

She took my hand and led me to the settee where we sat down. She pulled her legs up under her and got comfortable.

"I've got all night," she said.

I let out a deep sigh and resolved to tell her the truth about everything. I felt the need to unburden myself. No one on this planet knew my story. I had never discussed it with a single, solitary soul. Andi just sat there quietly, looking like an angel. I hoped she would be an angel of mercy.

I told her the whole sordid tale. I told her about meeting Laura, and falling in love for the first time since we had been together in college. I recalled our near perfect life together, and about our dream to buy a boat and run away to paradise together. When she asked what happened, I told her about Laura's death and my subsequent departure from reality. I admitted to taking money from my employer. I told her how I spent half of it on the boat, between the purchase and later repairs. I even admitted how I had blown the rest drinking in every bar between Punta Gorda and the Keys.

I told her about my little dope farming operation and my rum still. I told her about my customers and how it hadn't really worked out until just recently. When I described Cayo Costa she perked up a bit. She wanted to see it. I spilled my guts to her. Even as I spoke, I realized how pathetic it all sounded. I told her that I had not been with another woman since Laura, and how I worried that I was so broken I may never be with another woman again. I told her about Carol down in Marathon. She laughed at that story.

"At least one thing has changed about you," she said. "When I knew you, a naked chick in your bed would not have been turned away."

"True," I admitted, "But a lot has changed. I was a good husband. I wouldn't dream of ever cheating on Laura. I feel like being with another woman now; would be like cheating. I know it's not rational at this point, but there it is." I went on to explain how I thought about our college days often. I told her that I always considered her the one that got away. I had ached for her for years, but Laura had changed all that.

She stood up and paced around the salon. She was twirling her hair in her finger as she walked back and forth. Then she stopped and turned to face me.

"You've made a fine mess of your life, Meade Edwin Breeze," she said.

"I know, I know," I answered. "I can take you to land right now. I don't know where you live. I don't know your phone number. You can erase me from your life all over again if you want."

Instead of accepting that offer, she came to me and hugged me. It was very gentle. She rested her head on my chest and wrapped her arms around me.

"Will you let me help you?" she asked.

"Why would you want to do that?" I countered.

"It's like this, Breeze. A long time ago you thought I'd be ruining my life by marrying you. You wouldn't let me do that. I was young and stupid and horribly in love with you. I thought we could make it without Daddy's money, you and me against the world. You were the logical one, which was out of character for you. You spoke to me with that logic and it broke my heart. I went on to do what I was supposed to do, but I never forgot about you. I never married. There were plenty of men, some of them good men. They were not you. Don't turn me away again Breeze. I can help. I want to help."

I didn't see that little speech coming. When I arrived in town today, all I wanted was to get my little cash crop down to Marathon. If you had told me that I would run into Andi, and she would accept me in spite of my serious flaws, I'd have said you were crazy. The odds had to be a zillion to one. Then a thought occurred to me. I didn't really know what to say, so I stalled.

"Do you like rum?" I asked her.

"All pirates really do drink rum," she laughed. "I'll try some, thanks."

I delved into my secret stash of aged good stuff. I had almost forgotten about it. The last few runs from the still had been quite good. I learned that the longer it aged, the smoother it got. It had lost that first bite, but had maintained its sweet aftertaste. I poured us each a few ounces. I explained that it was my own special brew, Punta Blanca White. I raised a glass and made a toast.

"Here's to a most unlikely reunion."

We clinked glasses and took a sip. It was very nice.

"You made this?" she asked. "It's quite good."

We spent the next several hours talking. She had been a rising star at NASA. Everything was going great. She had it all. Slowly, she became dissatisfied with life. Was this all there was? She grew restless. She took stock of her life and decided it wasn't what she really wanted after all. She dropped out and moved to a cabin in Vermont for a few years. She read a lot of books and tried to write one of her own, but decided her life had been too boring to interest readers. The cold winters depressed her. Finally she packed a bag and caught a flight to Fort Myers. She had some money from her previous life saved up. She was tending bar a few days a week, going to beach, hitting the library and generally being a loafer.

I completely understood where she was coming from. I had dropped out too, just way harder and farther than her. I just shook my head, not believing that she was here on my boat.

"How'd you end up here in Fort Myers Beach, Andi?"

"You're going to think I'm crazy," she replied. "I had a dream, a silly dream that I'd find you here.

I was going stir crazy in Vermont, so I followed that silly dream, and here you are, in the flesh. Can you believe it?"

Right about then I didn't care if she said Moses had come down from a Vermont mountain and handed her stone tablets with my GPS coordinates. She was a gift from God, sent down to save my wayward soul. I couldn't say no to her.

"I hereby accept your offer of assistance," I stated in a formal tone. "But I have to tell you, Andi, I'm a broken man. I'm a wanted man. I'll let you help, but don't say I didn't warn you. I won't make the same mistake twice. I won't turn you away. I won't even say I told you so, when it all goes to hell."

"We shall see about that, Mr. Breeze," she said. "I think it was meant to be. So let's get on with it. Take me to Cayo Costa. Take me to Marathon. Show me your life."

We drank a little more rum while I explained about life aboard. I told her about water conservation and energy consumption. I told her about not having a real shower for weeks. I told her about incessant heat and mosquitoes at night. I also told her about glorious sunsets and crystal blue waters on white sand beaches. She declared herself not only willing, but eager to shove off.

It was almost four a.m. when we agreed we'd talked enough for one night. I gave her the bunk and said I would sleep on the settee. She took this as a chivalrous gesture. I didn't tell her that I actually preferred the settee and slept on it often. It was way too soon to think about sex, and it wasn't mentioned that night. I went to bed wondering how and when that bridge would be crossed. Laura's urn peered down at me from its perch on the dash. I quickly shut my eyes and kept them closed until I drifted off to sleep.

I dreamt of spreading Laura's ashes on the beach. In my dream it was something very urgent. I couldn't proceed with my life until I accomplished this task. I had previously thought that I'd someday spread the ashes on Jost Van Dyke. We had spent a wonderful day there, drinking painkillers at the Soggy Dollar Bar and hanging out with Foxy in Great Harbor. In my dream I was in the Bight at Norman's Island. The bar was Pirate's Cove, where we had shared a bucket of rum in chaise lounges on the water's edge. I lost the dream just as I was about to open the urn. It was still unfinished business, even in my dreams.

IT'S RAINING MONEY

W HEN I AWOKE THE NEXT morning, Andi was in the galley trying to figure out how to make coffee.

"There's no electricity," she shrugged.

"You have to turn on the inverter," I explained.

I showed her how, and gave her a quick lecture on energy consumption.

"You just use the inverter until the pot is done brewing, then you turn it off."

We sat on the aft deck, sipping Maxwell House and making our plans. She was excited for a new adventure. Dolphins rose to say good morning as the sun rose over the Key West Express. Shrimp boats eased off the docks and chugged their way towards the Gulf. I had this kind of morning every day, but having her there with me made it special. She really seemed to appreciate our surroundings.

"I could live like this," she said.

"You're about to get a taste," I told her. "Any time you want to return to land, just say the word."

"It's a deal, Breeze. No plans, no promises. Okay?"

That sounded fine with me. We sat quietly for a while longer. We discussed our departure and what needed to be done first. When she asked what to pack, I told her to bring sunblock, a few dresses for when we were in public, and bikinis, lots of bikinis. I also advised her to pick up a floppy hat if she didn't have one. She was not as tan as I was, and the Florida sun would cook her face and ears in minutes.

As I dropped her at the dinghy dock so she could go home and pack, I had the sudden fear that she wouldn't return. Maybe she was just showing me pity last night. I may never see her again.

"Bye, Andi," I called out as she walked up the ramp.

"I'll be back in one hour, Breeze," she said. "You just be here to pick me up."

One hour later, there she was, wearing a flowery sundress and a floppy hat. She carried just one small bag. God bless her. After we boarded the boat, she asked me where I kept my cash. I dug out the old coffee can from its secret hiding spot and opened it up. I still had a decent amount of cash from the pot party in Marathon. She pulled a wad of hundred dollar bills from her purse and stuffed it into the can.

"That should hold us for a little while," she beamed.

I felt like I was flush with money. I had no idea how this new episode in my life would turn out, but it was starting off nicely.

I needed to go through my checklist of routine maintenance items before we left. I told her to make herself at home, stow her stuff and get familiar with the boat. As I checked the oil and topped off the coolant, I could hear her going through the cabinets. I cringed a bit because I knew they were pretty bare. I climbed out of the bilge and wiped the grease from my hands.

"What are we going to eat?" she asked. "Spam and Dinty Moore?"

"You're in for a special treat," I countered. "We're taking the dinghy to Topps Supermarket. They've got the world's best Key Lime pie, and we'll stock up on whatever you want."

Actually, it would be a special treat for me. I hadn't really stocked up on food in a long time.

As we approached the landing behind Topps, we saw a vagrant sleeping in the grass. We had to step over him to make our way up the hill. He never stirred.

"I didn't realize there was such a seedy side to Fort Myers Beach," Andi said.

"Yea, it's one of the perks of living on the fringe of society," I answered. "I'm used to it. I deal with the bums in the park in Punta Gorda all the time. Just stay aware and don't act nervous. They're people too."

Encountering this particular bum made me eager to leave this town. There are no homeless people hanging out on the beach at Cayo Costa. We filled a cart with real food, even fruits and vegetables. I warned her that fresh produce doesn't stay fresh for long on a boat, but she was undeterred. She was going to eat healthy. I could eat out of a can if I wanted to. We stepped over the still-sleeping vagrant as we passed our bags across and loaded the dinghy.

I cranked up the engine as Andi put the groceries away. It was time to depart. Cayo Costa was over twenty-six miles to the north. I wanted to make it in time to show Andi a beautiful Gulf coast sunset. My heart was lighter than it had been in years. I had a childlike excitement in anticipation of a new adventure with this lovely woman. Would it all work out? Who knows? If it doesn't, well . . . that's just the way it goes. We were committed, and we were free.

We motored under the Matanzas Pass Bridge, out the Pass and into San Carlos Bay. I was grateful that my vessel's twenty-foot bridge clearance allowed us to go under the Sanibel Causeway. Taller boats had to go via the Punta Rassa route, adding five miles to the trip, and suffering through the Miserable Mile at the mouth of the Caloosahatchee River. I pointed out landmarks along the way. We passed the lighthouse at Point Ybel and entered the ICW near Saint James City. As we passed by Ding Darling Wildlife Refuge, Andi changed the topic of conversation. She asked about the urn.

"What's your long-term plan for her ashes?" she asked. "If you plan to hang on to the forever, just lugging them around with you, it's okay. I'm just curious."

I was relieved that she didn't lay some ultimatum on me about the urn. I'd expect any woman would feel weird having some dude's dead wife's ashes along for the ride every day. I told her about my original plan to take them to the BVI. I explained how the damage the boat suffered had set me back, and how my irresponsible use of money took care of the rest of it. It had, at first, been my reason for living, but I had failed. I kept on living, but still having the ashes was a continuing reminder of just how bad I had screwed things up. I didn't care about the embezzlement anymore, although it could still cause me to go to prison. I did carry a million pounds of guilt about the ashes though.

I even admitted to her about talking to the urn, and showing it the sunset. I was completely straight with her about my strange behaviors.

"That's not normal," she said, "But it's strangely romantic. You must have really loved her."

"I did indeed," I said. "It was so real and true. She was my life. I should feel even more guilty right now, for being with you. Instead I'm enjoying myself."

"That's good, Breeze. I am as happy as I can be. Let's just leave it at that for now. Let's just enjoy ourselves."

There was no more talk about Laura that day. She was wrapped in her towel, safely stowed away.

We crossed Pine Island Sound with Captiva Island to our port. Soon the ICW narrowed between Cabbage Key and Useppa Island. We could see Cayo Costa, but we had to continue north of Punta Blanca to find the entrance at Pelican Pass. I slowed to a crawl to navigate the narrow channel. I could see familiar faces on the sand spit to our starboard. On the beach was Jamie Brown, my seed supplier. He had a woman with him this time. Two other men were in the water with them. Looked like a party to me. I told Andi to go below and put on a bikini. As soon as we got settled on the anchor we'd join the fun.

I dropped the hook and set it good in the sand off Manatee Cove. As I finished putting the snubber on the anchor chain, Andi came out of the salon in a one-piece bathing suit. It was sheer and tight, but not particularly sexy.

"That's not a bikini," I commented with a chuckle.

"It's better than your run-of-the-mill bikini," she said. "It's a surprise. You'll like it. I promise."

We lowered the dinghy and set out to join the gathering on the beach.

Jamie had picked up a gal down in Key West. Her name was Char. She wasn't a bad-looking chick, especially for her age. She had mid-length blondish hair and wore a pretty small bikini. She was darkly tanned, with typical Florida wrinkle lines. She was nice enough, and seemed happy to have another woman join the group.

Jersey Tom had sailed his little Catalina out from Punta Gorda for a long weekend. He was a good friend of Jamie's. He had the whitest legs I'd ever seen in Florida. He turned out to be a great guy, but he seriously needed to wear shorts more often.

Oregon Rod had paddled his kayak to the beach. He lived aboard his twenty-seven foot Nor' Sea sailboat. It was a stout, blue-water-capable craft with classic lines. Both the boat and its owner had character. I liked characters. I'd run into plenty of them in my travels. After all the introductions were finished, I took off my shirt and waded out into the water to cool off. Andi joined me. We all drank beer, told stories, and drank in the Florida sunshine. We all started to leave the water, toweling off and sitting on the side of the dinghies. Andi was the last to come out.

Everyone stopped talking and every head turned. That non-descript bathing suit turned transparent when wet. It was completely see-through. Jamie and Tom lowered their sunglasses for an unfiltered look. Rod was a little less discreet.

"That's gotta be the sexiest thing I've ever seen," he blurted out. "My God woman, you're perfect." I couldn't disagree. She turned and gave him a little curtsy. Then she turned to me and asked if I liked it.

"What's not to like?" I answered. "Like Rod said, you're stunning in it. Not too many women of any age could pull that off."

"Thank you Breeze," she said. "I told you you'd like it."

I don't know what Char thought of the suit, but all the men were quite enjoying the view. Andi explained how it was all the rage in Monte Carlo. She picked it up in a boutique there while on vacation. The first time she had gone nude on the beach, she had burned all the parts that don't normally see the sun. The suit was SPF 30, and perfectly acceptable in the cafes, once dry. She wrapped a pretty sarong around her waist and donned her floppy hat. Rod asked if she didn't want to go for another swim, which gave us all a laugh. She was so comfortable in her own skin. She simply radiated beauty. I couldn't be more proud to be with her.

Eventually we ran low on drinks and the sun was getting low in the sky. The party broke up and we all returned to our respective boats for the night. Andi and I took a bit of rum out onto the bow to catch the last of the sunset. I thought about the Green Flash. I secretly apologized for cursing it before. My luck had certainly changed for the better. I dawdled a few extra minutes in case it decided to show itself again. It did not.

"That was a lot of fun," said Andi. "Is this how you live every day?"

"Actually, no," I answered. "I usually stay by myself. You know, keeping a low profile. I just thought you'd enjoy it. I had fun too."

"That's why we're here, Breeze, to enjoy ourselves."

I thought about that for a minute. Enjoyment hadn't been high on my list of priorities. I had a good time at Dockside, but kept to myself other than to talk with Carol and Miles. I worked the pot plants and the rum still. I worked on the boat. Mostly I wallowed in my grief, and my guilt. Having Andi aboard was changing that. After our talk about the urn, I hadn't thought of Laura again all day.

As we prepared to turn in for the night, I stretched out on the settee in my boxer shorts.

Andi stripped out of her suit and sarong there in front of me.

"Do you always sleep in those?" she asked.

"I usually sleep naked," I answered. "But I'm usually alone. Just trying to be polite to the lady."

"Don't you mind me," she said. "Sleep like you normally would. I won't bite. Besides, you've seen pretty much all of me today. It's only fair."

I made her turn her head. I dropped the shorts and stretched out again, covering myself with a light sheet. When she turned back around she laughed at me.

"Still hanging on to your modesty I see," she said.

"Trust me Andi. If I was as gorgeous as you, I'd run around naked all day long."

"You're so sweet, Breeze," she said. "Now go to bed. Good night and sweet dreams."

She blew me a kiss and disappeared into the bunk below, my bunk.

We spent the next week going to our own private beach every day. She wore a different bikini each time, telling me the see-through number was for special occasions only. Each day she would flaunt her nakedness for a short time. As much as I hated to see the suit go back on, I didn't want

133

those special parts to burn. She even talked me into skinny dipping in the broad daylight. I'd never done that in my life, but she had a way of getting what she wanted. Some afternoons we'd stop at Cabbage Key for a cheeseburger in paradise. We watched the sunset together every evening. We started holding hands as it sunk into the waters of the Gulf. We still had not broached the subject of sex.

At the end of that week a major physical change happened to me. I started waking up in the early morning with an almost painful erection. It was like cold, blue steel, and it was happening every day. Andi was asleep just a few feet away. Having her in my life, even though we barely touched, had reawakened a part of me long forgotten. I smiled to myself and welcomed Breeze Junior back to the game. I had a good suspicion that he would be put into service in the near future.

It happened just a few days later, but not in any way I could have predicted. Andi awoke before me and noticed the tent propped above my crotch. She decided to take matters into her own hands. I thought I was dreaming. Then she spoke.

"Good morning, Breeze, are you happy to see me, or is that a missile in your pocket?"

I tried to sit up but she gently nudged me back down. I stuttered some gibberish. My entire body tensed.

"Now now, just lay back and relax," she whispered. "Just let yourself go. Just enjoy."

Her touch was like velvet. Slowly she drew her fingers up and down the length of me. I couldn't protest. It was so gentle, her hands so soft. I wasn't even completely awake and I was glad for it. Under other circumstances I may have let my grief overcome me and screwed it up. Instead I gave in. I let out a long sigh and relaxed my body.

"That's good," she said, still whispering. "Let it all go. It's all right. Just let go."

And so I did. I let go in grand fashion. I let go all over myself and her hands, but she didn't stop.

"Let it go, Breeze. Let it all go."

I thought it would never end. I kept letting go. With it went the years of grief. With it went the years of guilt. It was the most basic of sexual acts, not perverted at all. It was almost innocent, like we were teenagers again. She was so selfless. She was so sweet. I hadn't done anything for her. I just laid there and let it go. When my spasms finally abated, one lone tear squeezed out of the corner of my eye. She kissed it off of my cheek. I could have burst out crying or sang hallelujah. My emotions ran from the pure joy of release at the hands of an angel, to a deep sadness for the loss of Laura.

I'd never be with Laura again. She was gone. Andi was here, and she was helping me to move on. I thought I'd never move on. I had fought hard not to move on. I had held on to Laura's memory with all of my being. Now here I was, letting go. Andi touched my face where the tear had been.

"Are you okay," she asked. "Is it Laura?"

"I am wonderful," I said. "I am wonderful. You are wonderful. And forgive me for being sad at the same time."

"I understand. You're going to be okay, Breeze. Let's just give it some more time."

She didn't return to me in the night like that again. She had taken me through a big step, and I guessed that she didn't want to push me too far, too fast. In the days that followed, she began to up the level of flirtation. We enjoyed trading sexual innuendos and playing grab ass, but we didn't take it further. We played in the surf. We basked in the sun. We drank ourselves silly. We had more parties on the sand spit with Jamie and Oregon Rod. She disrobed in front of me each night before leaving me to go to sleep alone.

I was really enjoying it. I didn't feel pressured into sex, but what we were doing was fun. On the other hand, there was something I was supposed to do, in order to take it to the next step. I obviously hadn't done it yet, whatever it was. I decided I should figure this little riddle out.

Instead I got distracted by the thought of all the dope I had stashed onboard. I should really call Tiki Terry down in Marathon and arrange to get rid of the stuff. Sure we had a good chunk of money between the two of us, but I didn't need to get caught with several pounds of weed. Forget about embezzlement and tax evasion, they would put me away for a long time. It's funny how I never worried about it before I found Andi. I didn't give a shit then. Now I was finally enjoying life. *Don't screw it up now, Breeze.*

I rarely made phone calls and no one ever called me. I left the phone turned off. The poor cell reception here always drained the battery. The easiest way to get a good signal was to take the dinghy down the ICW to Cabbage Key. I grabbed some cash to buy beer with, and we headed south on a flat, calm day. We beached the little boat on the sand to the left of the docks. After tying it up to the mangroves, we walked up the hill to the quaint little inn. I took a seat at the bar while Andi headed for the ladies room. As the phone powered up, I saw a notification that meant I had a voice mail. No one has this number, I thought. It was probably some telemarketer. I hated those notifications though, and the only way to get rid of them was to listen to the message.

I punched the buttons and put the phone to my ear. As soon as the voice started I remembered the one person who had this number. It was Mike Savage, the lawyer. The message was as follows: *Breeze, it's Mike Savage. You need to call me ASAP. There's an offer on the table. You can have a check within days if you accept. My advice is to take it. Call me.*

I sat there staring at the phone until it blinked out. I had totally put the whole legal case out of my mind. I never once thought about it. Now it was back. My thoughts turned to Laura. It was Laura money, but it was also my future. Maybe it's enough that I can quit selling dope, leave the country. My life was about to change dramatically.

So I called him back.

"Breeze, it's about time you called me," said Mike. "I'm about to make your day, I think."

"How much?" I asked.

"Two million to you after my firm takes one-third. I'm not taking half because we didn't go to court. We're not going to court, are we, Breeze?"

"No Mike, we don't need to go to court."

Just then Andi returned from the restroom.

"Can you hold on a minute Mike?" I asked.

I ran to Andi, picked her up and swung her around the bar next to the old piano. I put her down and did a little jig of my own. I hollered out, "Drinks are on me," for the whole place to hear. We were the only two in the bar besides the bartender. I picked the phone back up and told Mike I would accept. He asked where to send the check. That was a bit of a problem.

"Andi, do you have a bank account?" I asked.

"Of course," she answered. "Who doesn't?"

I let that pass and asked Mike if he could do a wire transfer.

"Sure Breeze, however you want it."

We gave him Andi's account information and he said the money would be wired within forty-eight hours. Andi still didn't know what was going on.

"Tell me, tell me," she insisted.

"I just made you a millionaire, pretty lady," I said. "In a few days, two million dollars is going to appear in your account. Help me spend a bunch of it."

"Is it legal?" she asked.

"All on the up and up, and tax free," I said. "Although I obviously need to keep it out of my name."

"This is so exciting, and sudden," she said. "What are you going to do with all? It won't last forever if you go all crazy with it."

"Let's sit down, have a few beers and think it over," I offered.

We sat there in the dark bar, under the big stuffed tarpon, and played everyone's favorite parlor game. What would you do if you won the lottery? I didn't care much for buying fancy things. *Leap of Faith* could use some upgrades. Hell, she could use a ton of upgrades. I was thinking farther in the future too. I should probably leave the country. Some third-world island paradise seemed nice. I've heard the American dollar goes a long way in Costa Rica, or maybe the Dominican Republic.

As I heard Andi discuss various charitable ventures, I worried about *Miss Leap*. She was old and tired. My little misadventure in Florida Bay gave me pause. I didn't think she could make it to the Caribbean. Just then Andi tugged on my sleeve.

"There's one thing you have to do, Breeze," she stated. "You need to complete your mission. Get Laura's ashes to the BVI."

She was right. I chastised myself for not immediately thinking the same thing. The past few weeks had been like a dream. I had been loving life, enjoying myself. I had not been the least bit focused on my supposed life's mission. I told her my concerns about my old boat. We agreed it was a problem. Crossing the Gulf Stream and traveling through the out islands of the Bahamas was serious business. It was potentially dangerous, and no place for a questionable vessel. I ordered two more beers and mulled over the predicament.

The more I mulled it over, the more urgent it became. I really needed to do this. I'd remain forever unfulfilled if I gave up. The money wouldn't buy my way out the regret. After adding a few shots of rum to my alcohol intake, I made a rash decision. I was real good at making rash decisions. They usually led to trouble, but I was quick to make them anyway. There at the bar on Cabbage Key, I told Andi my plan.

We'd take *Leap of Faith* back to Howie at the Marathon Boat Yard. I'd commission him to totally refurbish her. While the work was underway, we'd buy another boat. We'd get the best, blue-water-capable trawler money could buy. We'd cruise down through the Bahamas, Turks and Caicos, Dominican Republic, Puerto Rico, and finally, the BVI. It would be an adventure like no other. We'd see all the sights. We'd visit any cay we wished. We'd stop at fancy resorts if we wanted to. Money was no object. Once Laura's ashes were spread on the beach at Norman Island, we'd return to the states. I'd put the new boat up for sale and reunite with *Leap of Faith* in Marathon. She would be freshly refurbished by then, all shiny and new. I thought it was brilliant. Andi thought it was a complete misuse of my newfound fortune, but agreed anyway. She felt that fulfilling my pledge was the single most important thing. If I wanted to burn a million dollars doing it, it was my choice.

Andi had taken an interest in those ashes. It puzzled me. She was the one who reminded me when I forgot. She asked questions about Laura and our life together. We had talked about how she died, and how I reacted. She wanted to know all about our marriage. I told her everything. She had a certain manner of not only getting you to talk, but to really want to tell her everything. It was very therapeutic for me. I didn't understand why she cared. I had assumed that she would avoid the subject of ashes and dead wives. She did not.

Since she had been aboard, I hadn't talked to that urn once. I didn't bring it out to watch the sunset. Now I was closer than ever to actually spreading those ashes. I wasn't sure how I felt about that.

A NEW BOAT

OUR PLANNED DEPARTURE DAY FOR Marathon arrived. I awoke to a curious sight. Just outside the entrance to our anchorage sat both Fish and Wildlife, and the Lee County Sheriff's boats. I studied them through binoculars for a long time. Each boat that came or went was stopped. It was like a roadblock, except for boats. The channel was narrow and there was pretty much only one way out. It could have been safety checks, but the boats were free to go in just a few minutes.

We were completely ready to pull anchor and head south, but I wanted no parts of talking to law enforcement. They may have been there looking for me for all I knew. I had two options. I could stay put and hope they don't come inside the bay and start asking questions. I could risk leaving by the back door, which was an unmarked, winding little channel used by small boats with good local knowledge. I took a look at the tide prediction for that day. It would be at dead high in one hour. I had run it in the dinghy a hundred times, but the big boat needed four feet of water to keep her keel from touching bottom.

I explained the situation to Andi. She agreed we couldn't risk me being found, especially with two million dollars on the line. I fired up the engine, pulled anchor and very slowly eased *Leap of Faith* towards the questionable channel. I knew the way, I just didn't know if we'd have enough water. We inched alongside a prominent sand bar that protruded into the bay from Cayo Costa. I looked down at less than a foot of water, only a few feet from our hull. We crawled along at one knot, waiting to run aground. Andi kept an eye on the lawmen with the binoculars. They were still stopping runabouts. I feared that if we grounded, they would come to investigate. Just as we started to swing to port and into deeper water, I felt the bottom rubbing. I took it out of gear, and we eased to a slow stop. We were in soft sand and the water was clear enough to see bottom. I had turned a few feet too soon. Our overall length of thirty-six feet was just a tad too long to make the curve in the channel. The tide was still rising, but would peak in less than half an hour.

I decided to step off the boat and walk out in front of her to check depths. The water was only up to my chest. Slightly to starboard the depth dropped just a bit. I made Andi unpin the anchor and lower it down to me. I carried it out away from the bow as she played out more chain. Fifty feet away the water was up to my chin. I dropped the anchor there. I was glad I had taken the time to finally fix the windlass. As so often happens on a boat, it was simply a matter of corroded connections. Back on board I gave the windlass a few bumps. We moved forward six inches. I repeated the process again, gaining us a foot. The bottom of our keep was just resting on the bottom, not dug in. We just need a few inches more water and we'd float free. The windlass was really groaning under the strain. I hoped it would hold up.

Finally we floated. Our keel now had almost six inches clearance above the sand. I called for Andi to winch the anchor up as we moved forward. I couldn't let us drift while I hauled anchor and ran up to the helm, we could drift aground again. It worked. We eased off into deeper water and turned hard to port to follow the channel over towards

Punta Blanca. We rounded a sandy point, passed by the remains of an old fish house and entered the ICW just off of Useppa Island. We both kept looking aft for law enforcement, but they never showed. I had pulled it off. I secretly apologized to *Miss Leap* for scratching her bottom paint. I gave the control panel a pat. *Good job old girl.*

We motored down the ICW until we reached San Carlos Bay. I then aimed us southwest, out into the Gulf.

"We're not stopping in Fort Myers Beach?" asked Andi.

"I want to put some miles between us and those cops. We can make Marco in time for happy hour if we keep on plugging."

We dropped anchor in Factory Bay around seven p.m. Happy hour was a little late, but we made up for lost time. We toasted *Miss Leap*. We toasted Mike Savage. We toasted Laura's ashes. I didn't remember going to sleep, but I woke up alone on the settee. I started the coffee pot and sat down to look over the charts for south Florida and Florida Bay. It would take ten hours to make Little Shark River, which I wanted to avoid. Marathon was another eight if we made good time. I'd save maybe two hours by skipping the approach to

Little Shark. So I figured sixteen hours to Boot Key Harbor. If we left at midnight, we might make it to the boatyard before they closed the next day at five.

It was Andi's first offshore experience and she loved it. The waters below Marco Island are Caribbean clear. It was almost flat and we made good time. The old boat chugged along all night and most of the next day. We made Marathon before four o'clock that afternoon. Howie's dockhands grabbed our lines and we settled in to our slip. Howie himself came down to greet us.

"What is it this time, Breeze?" he growled. "You bust this old tub up again?"

"Nope," I said. "She's just fine old man. Lock up your office and I'll buy you a beer. I've got a long list for you."

We all went off to party at the Dockside. Howie would stare at Andi for a minute, then turn and look at me. We ordered our drinks and finished up with the pleasantries. Then I got down to business.

"I am entrusting you the future of *Leap of Faith*, Howie," I said. "Do you accept a commission to supervise her complete restoration?"

"I don't know Breeze," he answered, scratching his chin. "You're talking a whole lot of money. That boat's no spring chicken."

"Trust me," I countered. "I can cover it."

"What'd you find floating this time, a bunch of coke?"

"Ha ha ha, Howie," I said. "It's all legit. Maybe I wrote a book and it became a best seller."

"That would be the day," he laughed. Then he laughed some more, really howling. It was contagious. I started laughing. Andi started laughing. People around us in the bar started laughing at us.

"Bartender, bring us another round," I yelled out. I noticed Carol wasn't anywhere to be seen.

Finally we pulled ourselves together as more beers arrived. I pulled a handwritten list out of my pocket.

"This is what I want done," I said. "And I've got fifty grand to get you started. If it goes over that, I'm good for it."

He let out a low whistle as he read the list.

1. Complete electrical system replacement, including batteries.
2. New engine, preferably the American Diesel 135.

3. Complete paint job.
4. Interior redesign with all new appliances.
5. New electronics, to include radar and autopilot.
6. New canvas and Eisenglass.
7. All teak refinished.
8. Any associated parts or systems that needed upgrading; such as starter, alternator, transmission, raw water pump, bilge pumps, etc.

"I want the best of everything, Howie," I said. "The best contractors, the best paint, the best parts."

"It's gonna take a long time you know. Yours ain't the only boat we got to work on."

"I'll give you a year," I said. "We're leaving the country for a while."

"You sure you didn't find some coke?" he asked.

We all started laughing again. Eventually we shook hands and pushed back our stools to leave. We needed an early start the next day to get to Miami.

"You take good care of my baby," I yelled across the parking lot.

"Ya won't recognize her when you come back, Breeze," he yelled back.

I felt like I was leaving her in good hands.

The next order of business was to call Tiki Terry. He agreed to come pick us up, after dark. I loaded my dusty old backpack and whatever bags I could find with the pot. We transferred it over to Terry with no money exchanged. I told him to sell it or smoke it or whatever he wished. He could keep whatever cut he felt was fair. Someday I'd come back and we would settle up. Who knew when that would be?

We walked out onto US 1 and found a rundown motel for the night. When the clerk asked if I wanted a single king or two queens, Andi piped in and selected two beds. I shrugged my shoulders and paid the man, in cash. We sat in our shabby room that night and discussed the day's events.

"You really love that old boat," she said. "You love her like you loved your wife. That's why you won't just sell her and just keep the new boat."

"I guess you could say that. She has been all I have for a long time. She's special to me. Without her I'd be just another bum in the park. Would you have agreed to help if you found me asleep in the grass behind the Topps market?"

"I would have," she said, which surprised me. "But I see you pilot that thing like a seasoned sea captain. I see you checking her systems and fixing things yourself. I saw you give her a pat when we got unstuck."

"And you saw me give Howie fifty grand to make her new," I said.

"Kinda crazy when you are buying a new boat," she answered. "It's your money. A fool and soon parted and all that."

"It's like this," I said. "That boat wasn't my dream alone. Laura and I shared the dream together. We even picked the name together. I feel somehow close to her when I'm on that boat. Like maybe she is looking down on me. I know she's not in that urn. If she was, I couldn't spread them. I can part with the ashes, but I'll never part with our boat."

That ended our conversation for the night. She got up, turned off the lights and tucked in to her bed with giving me the benefit of watching her undress.

The next day we took the shuttle up the Overseas Highway and into Miami. The mass of tall buildings and urban sprawl overwhelmed me. The beach must have had a million people on it. Not my kind of town.

The broker was happy to see us walk into his office. He smelled a big commission. He was dressed like an exaggerated version of a yachtsman. He smiled a lot, called me "Mr. Breeze", and seemed eager to please. Beneath all that, I sensed a former used-car salesman. Some lucky break got him promoted to yacht broker in Miami, or maybe his father-in-law felt pity for him and gave him a job. It didn't matter, I was buying a boat. Let him make his money.

Broker Dan asked a bunch of questions about my boating experience and tried to angle them in such a way that he could figure out my financial status. I told him my current yacht was currently undergoing a complete restoration at the Marathon Boatyard. That seemed to satisfy him. He lead us down the docks to see what we came to see.

There floating in a slip with a carpeted gangway and velvet ropes, floated a magnificent vessel. She was a brand new Grand Banks 47 in the Europa style. Its lines were a lot like *Leap of Faith's*, but everything about her was pristine. She had big twin diesels, a bow and stern thruster, and all the bells and whistles. Her big generator would power all three of her air conditioning units. The guest stateroom was bigger than my old salon, while the master stateroom could house a football team. The head and shower were luxurious, like a five-star hotel.

She had huge water tanks and fuel tanks, which gave her tremendous range. At low RPMs, traveling at eight knots, it would sip just six gallons per hour. It had the capacity to run twenty-five knots, but would gulp fuel at that speed. It was the ultimate long-range trawler, and it was a thing of beauty.

We spent two hours crawling all over her. Broker Dan grew impatient. He asked if I wanted to arrange a sea trial, which was a sure way of moving the negotiations along. A sea trial would require some earnest money, and an offer would be expected. I asked how much he needed down in order for us to get a sea trial. His answer was twenty percent, much higher than I figured. I had put down ten percent when I was buying *Miss Leap*.

"I tell you what Dan-o," I said. "I'll give you half down if you let me have a two week sea trial. I want to take it out at anchor and use all her systems thoroughly. If everything goes well, I'll pay the balance in two weeks. Your guys can fix anything that breaks or needs tweaking when I bring it back."

He stuttered and stammered and said he had to check with the owner of the brokerage.

"I'm not negotiating on this," I said. "I'll pay full asking price, no haggling. Just let me have my extended trial and it's a deal."

He left the room for a good fifteen minutes. When he returned he had the boss man with him. He looked me up and down, probably not believing that I had the funds. I had worn my best shirt for the occasion, but he was not impressed. I thought maybe it was time for a new best shirt. That's when Andi stepped in. She was wearing a sexy little sundress that rose dangerously high on her thighs when she swung around.

She introduced herself and explained that she was the one who would actually be writing the check. She touched his arm. She tucked her chin into her shoulder and twirled her hair in one finger. Her coy smile melted the old bastard. He excused himself to draw up some papers. We should be able to finalize the settlement when we returned in two weeks. I imagined him in the other room checking into her account balance somehow.

I asked Dan-o if we could stay on her in the slip tonight so I could get familiar with the controls.

"Whatever you like, Mr. Breeze," he said. "I've never seen my boss act like that around a woman. We get plenty of lookers through here."

"Yea, she has a way. Believe me, she has a way."

She came down the docks to the boat arm in arm with the owner. He had a huge smile on his saggy old face. He helped her up the ramp and she winked at me as she stepped aboard. He was the one who needed help. I wondered if she was just leading me around by the arm. We spent that evening drinking champagne in air-conditioned comfort aboard our new yacht. I picked up a chart book for The Keys at the local West Marine and studied likely anchorages. Andi had written a check for one hundred and seventy thousand dollars. At settlement, we would pay the rest of the eight hundred and fifty thousand dollar total balance. Almost half of the money would be gone, but I'd make a good portion of it back when we sold the new boat a year from now.

"I have to give you my heartfelt thanks, Miss Mongeon," I said to Andi. "You signed on to a hopeless cause. There was no way for you to know I was about to come into money. I didn't even know. You came along for the ride anyway. Things have turned around now. I owe you a debt of gratitude."

"Charity has its rewards Breeze," she replied. "Thank you for showing me a different life."

When bedtime arrived, I didn't offer the master stateroom to Andi. I couldn't picture such a petite woman sleeping all alone on that king-sized mattress. She took it anyway, leaving me the perfectly adequate guest bunk. It was still much nicer than what I was used to. I thought that it was the perfect night to consummate our relationship. She thought differently. Instead she disrobed in front of me as usual, kissed me on the lips, and said good night. I admired her ass as she walked away, recalling the one night that she had come to my bed.

The next morning, I had one more piece of business to take care off before we shoved off. I asked Dan-o about hiring someone to put a new name on the back of the Grand Banks. Of course, he had a recommendation. Gail from *Names on Boats* could be there within the hour. She showed me some fonts and colors. She measured the transom, taking her shoes off before stepping out onto the teak swim platform. She wanted four hundred bucks for the job, but promised it would be of the most professional quality in Florida. For an extra hundred she could have it done by noon and return to install it after lunch. I accepted her terms. By mid-afternoon, the work was finished. The Grand Banks was ready for christening. Her new name was *Ashes Aweigh*.

THE BAHAMAS AND BEYOND

WE SPENT OUR TWO-WEEK TRIAL hopping around The Keys, mostly on the Florida Bay side. We raised and lowered the anchor with the boat's powerful new windlass. I kept an eye on the battery banks, but we ran the generator plenty to keep things charged up. I inspected the engine room daily, checking for leaks at thru-hulls, looking for dripping oil, anything that would need to be addressed prior to settlement. All systems were working perfectly. I especially enjoyed running on autopilot. Look Ma. No hands!

Andi wowed the tourist and staff when we made an appearance at the Lorelei. She wore that one particular sundress with the dangerously high hemline. I thoroughly enjoyed the spectacle. Men and women alike couldn't stop staring at her. As we sat outside at the tiki bar, I recalled how I was once a regular giver of thanks for all of my good fortune. I had lost that, but now was an appropriate time to start the ritual again. I had just stepped off an expensive new yacht, taken my fancy tender in to a popular spot in The Keys, and made a grand entrance with a stunning beauty on my arm. Life had gotten good again. I looked up at the sky and said a silent prayer that it would continue.

In Key West, we paid the ridiculous slip fee at the Galleon Resort Marina. With it came the use of all the amenities the resort had to offer. My escort wore her tiniest bikini to the pool and again I was the envy of every man around us. She wanted to shop on Duvall. She hadn't really packed much in the way of clothes. She hadn't bought anything for herself the entire time. She told me that my wardrobe could use an upgrade as well. I hated shopping. I did however, enjoy drinking beer. I told her to shop all she wanted. She could find me a new best shirt while I sat in The Bull waiting for her.

When she found me at the bar, she carried just two shopping bags. She had bought a few new dresses, a sheer cover-up to put on over bathing suits, and a cute little pair of sandals. They were so small you could hang them from your rearview mirror. I praised her frugality. Most women with a blank check would have bought out every shop on Duval. Then again, I had spent almost a million dollars in the past two weeks.

We watched the sunset celebration from Mallory Square. She put five bucks in the tip jars of every street performer. Charity has its rewards, she reminded me. We spent a lazy afternoon at Schooner's Wharf, listening to Michael McCloud sing and play. He was really getting old. He looked to be in poor health. His dog, who didn't look too spry either, slept in his guitar case the entire show. He could still perform though. The old guy could pick and sing with the best of them, in my opinion.

Finally, our time ran out. We took Hawk Channel and put the hammer down for Miami. I wanted to push the new boat a little. We had been just puttering along at low RPMs, allowing the new engines a breaking-in period. I couldn't believe the power it had. It wasn't a hull that really planed, but it did lift up in the water a bit and level out nicely. We zipped along incredibly fast for such a big, heavy boat, and made Biscayne Bay in no time at all. When we had left that first day, I was nervous maneuvering something so big. Now that I had gotten familiar with the twin-engine controls and the thrusters, docking was a snap. I thought about calling Marathon and having a bow thruster installed on *Leap of Faith*.

We came to a perfect stop and the dockhands took our lines. The owner was expecting us, and everything was in order to close out the sale. I asked for a larger main anchor, and a better suited secondary anchor for use in the Bahamas. A mechanic went on board to make some adjustments, but overall the boat was perfect. Andi went inside with the lecherous old owner and took care of the formalities. We were ready to set sail for the Caribbean.

We crossed Biscayne Bay and staged in an attractive anchorage some three hundred and fifty yards off the westerly shores of Sands Key. We'd wait for a suitable weather window before attempting to cross the Gulf Stream. As we readied for our nightly sunset viewing, I asked Andi if she really wanted to do this.

"It's going to be a long trip," I told her. "If you want to bail I can take you back to Miami. Just say the word."

"If you will have me, I'd like to finish what we started," was her answer. "I worry about you and those ashes. I want to see this through. I have no idea what happens afterward, but for right now, you are going to finish your mission. I'm in."

So it was settled. We were really going to do this. I hadn't thought about what would happen afterwards either. Would we make a life together? I still had those embezzlement and tax evasion charges hovering out there somewhere. Andi and I were not lovers, at least not in the physical sense. Too many unanswered questions fogged my mind. I decided to put it all aside and concentrate on our upcoming adventure instead. The weather was right and the boat was ready.

We left at first light. Exiting the bay just south of Fowey Rocks, I set a course for due east, even though Bimini was slightly to the north. The strong current in the Gulf Stream would carry us several degrees north. If I miscalculated, we had plenty of power to make adjustments on the fly. *Leap of Faith* would have had problems fighting the current and a more exact reckoning would have been called for. In *Ashes Aweigh*, we could make the fifty-mile trip in five hours or less, depending on how hard I wanted to push her. Ten knots seemed to be her sweet spot, so I settled on that.

Sure enough, five hours later we were approaching the channel between North and

South Bimini. I slowed to make sense of the confusing markers. Dead ahead was a shallow bar. There were two channels. To starboard lay a set of markers leading into South Bimini, and Bimini Sands Marina. To port, the channel continued on to North Bimini with a host of marinas and services. I selected Bimini Blue Water Resort in Alice Town Harbor. After docking we checked in with Customs and Immigration. We paid for our six-month cruising permit and retired to the bar at The Anchorage Restaurant. Cheers to a successful crossing. It had been a calm and uneventful day. That great big ocean had been a millpond for us. We were off to a good start.

Back aboard I checked the weather and plotted a course across the Great Bahama Bank. It would be a very long day. If all went well and the weather was good, we could just barely make it around the NorthWest Channel mark and into Chub Cay before dark. I did not want to anchor out on the open waters of the Bank overnight, although some slower boats did so successfully.

"Well, what did you think?" I asked Andi.

"It was wonderful, but a little spooky too," she said. "The whole time that we couldn't see land was a little unnerving, but exciting at the same time."

"I'm just glad it was calm," I told her.

"That's because my super smart captain picked a good day," she said. "Why do I feel like I can trust your judgment so much? You seemed to have made all the wrong turns in life, but when it comes to running a boat, you're a pro."

"I think I'll take that as a compliment," I said. "A boat has been my refuge from the consequences of all my poor choices. Make any sense?"

"I can see that," she answered. "Just keep us on the right course going forward."

"Aye aye, first mate," I said, as I saluted smartly.

We made it across the bank in plenty of time. I anchored us off the Chub Cay Club. We were in the Bahamas, but so far we hadn't seen much. Bimini was a bit rundown looking, like everything had been built in the seventies. The Grand Bahama Bank offered little scenery except blue water. As we approached Frazers Hog Cay, it was hard to tell where it ended and Chub Cay began. Finally I noticed all the masts from the marina, and located the telltale water tower. We planned to spend just one night, moving on to New Providence and Nassau Harbor in the morning. It was the last good stop for fuel, water and provisions for a long time. As I worked the charts, Andi looked over my shoulder. She wanted to spend some time in Nassau. The Atlantis Resort was something she wanted to see.

"This is like a vacation for me," she said. "I want to see the sights and enjoy myself as much as possible, not just head straight down the islands every day." I didn't argue. Let her have a little fun. We had enjoyed great weather the past several days and I had hoped to take advantage of the steady forecast the next few days. Instead, we'd hang out in Nassau for awhile.

Entering Nassau Harbor was an exercise in sensory overload. We had to share space with huge cruise ships, Haitian boats under sail, seaplanes landing and taking off, and all manner of recreational and fishing vessels going to and fro. I radioed the harbor master to advise him of our intentions. He advised me to take a direct route to our chosen marina and not to tarry in the traffic lanes.

Atlantis Resort dominated not only Paradise Island, but the entire Nassau waterfront district. It was a sheer mass of coral sand pink with high bridged towers, spires, cupolas, domes and leaping sailfish. Andi thought it was magnificent. I thought it the gaudiest piece of architecture I had ever seen.

I had to admit though, the size and scope of such a massive and intricate building was stunning.

I had chosen East Bay Marina because it was reasonably priced. I hadn't completely forgotten how poor I'd been the past few years. It was also right next to the bridge to Paradise Island, and a short walk to Atlantis. Atlantis had its own marina, but it was lined with mega-yachts and was very expensive. East Bay had dockhands at the ready and we found them very friendly. As we chatted on the dock I slipped each a ten dollar bill, pulling them from a wad of cash in my pocket. A jet-black Bahamian dockhand pulled me aside. He advised I not show so much money in public, and to stick to the tourist district. Don't stray into Nassau for more than a few blocks: after that, crime was rampant. I thanked him and took his advice to heart.

It had been a short, easy trip, and Andi couldn't wait to start exploring. As we crossed the bridge onto Paradise Island, Atlantis rose before us like a space-age temple. It was even more impressive up close. It was dynamic and eye popping in its colors, angles and curves. Tourists scrambled all over.

"Let's hit the casino," squealed Andi. "This is so exciting."

I'd been in casinos before, but this was something different. It was huge and everything was new and shiny. It was another case of sensory overload for me, as bells and whistles and sirens rang out from all directions. Loud music came from the main stage. Andi pulled me along as I tried to take it all in. We stopped in front of three special slot machines. For one hundred bucks you got one spin. The digital readout above said that the current winning jackpot was almost one million dollars.

"Go ahead, Breeze," urged Andi. "You've been on a roll lately. Give it a shot."

I pulled out two bills, giving one to her.

"If you win, keep the cash," I told her. "It's yours."

We each pushed our buttons and waited in anticipation as the wheels spun. I crapped out on my machine. I watched as her spinning wheels came to a stop. She crapped out too. Two hundred bucks down the drain.

We left the gaming area and found the aquarium, although the word "aquarium" is insufficient to describe it. Glass-sided tunnels carried over reefs. Tanks centered around the Atlantis Dig were an archaeological fantasy. We lingered for hours.

Finally we decided we were hungry and set out to find a restaurant. There were about a dozen of them. We chose Fathoms and sat down to a wonderful fish dinner. I hadn't eaten fresh-caught fish in a while. I decided I should troll a line from now on when we were underway. Our bill came and we left a hefty tip. Another hundred bucks down the drain. The rest of our Nassau experience would be more of the same. I watched helplessly as we paid hundred-dollar dinner bills, hundred-dollar bar tabs, and hundred-dollar boutique charges.

Andi was having the time of her life, but we stayed way too long. When I finally talked her into leaving, the weather outside the harbor turned bad. Strong northerlies had set in, building huge swells in the offshore waters. We were stuck for another week. A lot more hundred dollar bills disappeared.

Finally, we had a weather window. I was anxious to break free of all congestion, high rises, and noise of Nassau. We set out early for Allan's Cay in the northern Exumas. I enjoyed being back at the helm of such a fine vessel. The realization that I was the owner and captain of a nearly million-dollar ship made me chuckle. I was carting one of the world's most desirable women around the Bahamas. I'd just dropped over ten thousand dollars eating and drinking in Nassau. Not too many months ago I was eating half a can of Spam for dinner.

As soon as we dropped anchor at Allan's Cay, I suddenly felt insufficient. There were several super yachts anchored before us. One of them had to be two hundred feet long. It was the kind of ship only a multi-billionaire would own. Uniformed crew scurried about serving drinks and shining stainless. It was almost as impressive as Atlantis.

"My God, Breeze," said Andi. "Who do you think it is?"

"It's either Mick Jagger or a Saudi prince," I guessed. "I am suppressing my envy. I wouldn't trade *Leap of Faith* for that garish-looking example of conspicuous consumption."

"Do I detect a hint of jealousy?" she asked.

"If they had the pleasure of feasting their eyes on you, they would be jealous of me," I replied.

"You're so kind, Breeze, but they probably have a boatload of pretty girls."

"It doesn't matter," I said. "I still wouldn't trade places."

She smiled that smile and took my hand. We sat on the aft deck and watched the sun set over the mega-yachts. I went back to feeling pretty good about myself. The next day we moved a few miles south to Highborne Cay for a more unobstructed view. We had the anchorage to ourselves. Andi never dressed that day. She simply walked around deck nude, alternating between sun and shade. Her tan was progressing nicely.

We spent a few days at Normans Cay anchored near a partially submerged airplane. I pictured a desperate drug-runner ditching in the lagoon. We explored in the tender until we found a place called McDuff's on the southern end of the island. My cheeseburger was awesome, but it caused a Jimmy Buffett song to be stuck in my head for the rest of the day.

At Warderick Wells we anchored in some of the clearest water we had yet seen. A four-foot barracuda hung in the shade of our swim platform. Lemon sharks swam by. It was so totally peaceful and quiet, we could hear birds singing from the island. We saw the ruins of an old settlement off Rendezvous Beach, and another on Hawksbill Cay. We sat in the water at Beryl's Beach for hours, enjoying the sheltered beach. We walked to the top of Boo Boo Hill where I stuck a Leap of Faith sticker on a wooden post next to all the other mementos left by previous visitors. The view from atop the hill was simply amazing.

Our next stop was Sampson Cay. We drove the tender over to Fowl Cay for an elegant dinner at the Hill House. It was the first time I got to wear my new best shirt that Andi bought for me back in Key West. After dinner we took our cocktails out onto a spectacular terrace overlooking the water. We moved over to Staniel Cay where we dove Thunderball Cave. We enjoyed dinner at the Staniel Cay Yacht Club before going over to Big Major's Cay to see the wild pigs. We stopped off at Cave Cay for a few days before making the jump down to Georgetown. It may have been the most scenic stopover yet.

Each time we moved the boat to a new location, we had good weather. The trips were short hops and we never ran into trouble of any kind. I only transited on near perfect weather days. Each place was so beautiful, if didn't matter if we were stuck for a few more days. The water was so clear, it was easy to see the coral heads and steer around them. The sun shone and the winds were light. Life was a perpetual following sea. That was about to change.

CHICKEN HARBOR

WE COULD HAVE CONTINUED HOPPING around in these Cays for months, but we were running low on just about everything. We needed a viable harbor with fuel, water, trash disposal and groceries. I had gotten very comfortable piloting these waters and reading the weather, too comfortable. The run from Cave Cay to Georgetown Harbour was a much longer one. Our weather was fine. Georgetown's weather was fine. I completely missed a nasty little system further off shore.

We needed to go a bit off shore to avoid some charted reefs and we ran right into it. Thirty knots easterlies built the seas incredibly high. We were taking huge waves on our port bow. Each pounding conspired to throw us off course, and the autopilot refused to cooperate. As I watched a particularly large set of waves approach, I turn our bow head-on into them. *Ashes Aweigh* rode up and over the first two, then smashed through the third. Salt water a foot deep ran down the decks and fought to escape through the scuppers. We took the spray up on the fly bridge like someone had thrown a bucket of water on us. Andi screamed.

"What are we going to do?"

"Put your life jacket on now," I yelled above the roar of the wind and waves. "Inside that compartment is a bright yellow bag. It's a ditch bag, just in case."

"Should we call the Coast Guard or something?" she asked. I could hear the fear in her voice.

"You're not in Kansas anymore, my pretty," I said. "There is no Coast Guard out here. We'll be okay."

She wasn't so sure. The radar showed that we'd pull out of the worst of it in a few more miles. Meanwhile, the torrential rain was coming sideways and the winds were up to forty knots. An odd wave turned us sideways and we took a big one directly on our port side. The boat lay over hard on its starboard side. The starboard rail went under. Andi screamed again as she fell over into me. Our heavy keel caused us to snap-roll back upright, throwing her back to the other side of the boat. I was ejected from the helm seat and landed on top of her. She was curled up on the deck sobbing.

When I regained the wheel, the boat was almost stern-to. I hollered "hold on", and I spun the wheel and gassed the throttles. I almost had the bow into the next wave when it broke completely over the rail and submerged the front third of the boat. We popped back out of it like a submarine surfacing. This was not good. Who knows what kind of damage that much water was going to cause. I looked out over the vicious looking sea. It was damn ugly. I cursed Poseidon. I cursed the Green Flash. I cursed myself. I had gotten cocky and failed to respect the power of the ocean. I asked God for mercy on my foolish soul.

I held the bow into the oncoming waves even though we were headed in the wrong direction. I found somewhat of a rhythm. I'd add some throttle going up the face, then slow the engines as we dropped off on the other side. I looked over at Andi sitting on the floor in her own vomit. Up and down we went. I heard things crashing around down below. The sight of Andi's predicament made me queasy. She had a white-knuckle grip on a grab rail. She was soaking wet with more than just seawater. She was crying uncontrollably. *Way to go Breeze. You're a real pro.*

All I could do was hang on. Eventually the seas became more manageable. When I determined that the autopilot would hold us on course, I went below to get some towels and rags. I stepped through a minefield of broken dishes and assorted debris thrown about the cabin. Back on the bridge, I helped Andi up into her seat and cleaned her up. She put on a fresh blouse and I held her tight.

"I'm so sorry," I said. "But it's okay now. We're going to be okay."

She laid her head on my chest and said, "I never, ever, want to do that again."

The sky brightened and the winds died. We had wandered off course pretty far. I pointed us in the proper direction and calculated our time of arrival. We'd make it well before dark, but the sun would be lower in the sky, making reading the water depths more difficult.

Just as we neared the entrance, I got confused. There were no markers. I had read up on this route, but I apparently had forgotten some of it. At Conch Cay Cut there was a reef on my port side. As I cleared the first reef and turned a bit to port, another reef appeared to starboard. I headed for Simon's Point and paralleled the coast of Great Exuma for about a half-mile. I picked up the Stocking Island beacon and turned to port. Apparently, I turned too soon. We ran aground just outside the unmarked channel. *You're on a roll today Breeze.*

Fortunately it was soft sand. In short order some of the locals came out in small boats to pull us off. It didn't make me feel any better when they said this happens all the time. For the first time since our reunion, Andi was in a foul mood. Her fear had transformed into anger, and it was directed at me.

"You get me off this boat," she yelled at me. "You get me off this boat right now. I'm going to a hotel. I'm booking a flight, and I'm flying back to Florida."

Instead of opening my mouth and saying something stupid, I went to her and held her tight. She started crying again.

"I thought we were going to die out there," she whimpered. "I've never been so terrified in my life. I'm no salty sailor like you are, Breeze."

"Believe me," I said. "I was just as terrified as you. Please forgive me. The last thing I want to do is put you in harm's way."

"It was horrible," she said. "I don't think I can go out there again."

"We're safe now," I said. "We made it. The boat made it. We're fine."

"I am not fine," she countered. "I'm tired, I'm bruised, and my dignity has taken a beating."

My eloquence escaped me. Not knowing what to say, I headed for the liquor cabinet. When in doubt, drink. (Maybe not the best rule for everyone, but it has served me well.) I found several broken bottles and a fine mess of booze and glass. Plan B. I went to the fridge and got two cans of beer. As soon as I handed her a beer, I slugged down half of mine in one long pull.

"Looks like we have a mess to clean up," I told her. "I'm going to go survey the rest of the damage." She gave me a look I couldn't interpret. It wasn't one I had seen before. It was a long way from the chin-tucking, hair-curling look.

What I found was one wet boat. Everything forward of mid-ship was soaked. Boats are designed to keep the water out, but they are not designed to be partially submerged. During those few seconds when we nosed underneath a big wave, water had found its way in. Water always wins. The bedding was damp. Towels, clothes, and toilet paper were all sopping. It would take a long time to dry out. I fired up the big generator and turned on all the air-conditioners. They would help to dehumidify things. I carried all the wet stuff out on deck and draped it over every available perch. I found some dry towels in an upper storage compartment and mopped up any standing water. Then I hung the towels over the rail to dry.

Andi stopped pouting and joined in the effort. We spent all afternoon cleaning up broken glass and mopping up moisture. When our traditional five-o'clock happy hour approached, I called an end to the work detail. We decided to launch the tender and take a look around the harbor. Over at Stocking Island, cruisers were playing volleyball on the beach. We saw a sign that said Hamburger Beach under a tall monument. We continued winding through the hundreds of anchored boats until we came to a well-protected and somewhat isolated cove. According to the guidebook, this was called Redshanks. I liked it. I decided to pull up anchor and relocate *Ashes Aweigh* to this quiet cove.

We pulled into Redshanks with all our assorted wet stuff flying in the breeze. It was like redneck laundry day. It was quite a way to introduce ourselves. I didn't even get the anchor fully set when we were approached by a man in a tender. He introduced himself as Captain Fred. He lived aboard a seventy-foot Hatteras named *Incognito*. He was the unofficial commodore of the Redshanks Yacht and Tennis Club. I looked, but no tennis courts were to be found. The RSYTC turned out to not really be a yacht club at all, but rather an informal moniker taken by those that anchored here.

Captain Fred was not a big man. He stood maybe five foot, six inches. He was nearly bald with a three-day beard. He chewed an unlit cigar constantly. He looked around at all the wet blankets, sheets and towels.

"Ya have a bit of trouble coming in did ya?" he asked.

Andi piped in, "Breeze tried to kill us out there. I'm lucky to be alive."

"We got caught in a storm," I said. "It was kind of hairy for a while, but we survived."

"Welcome, then, to Redshanks," Fred said. "It will be nice to have such a pretty lady in attendance. Nothing but old biddies on the beach here lately."

He took Andi's hand and gave it a gentlemanly kiss. He got a curtsy in return.

Captain Fred became my mentor and tour guide after that. He showed me where to do our laundry, get groceries, buy booze and introduced me to those he thought I should know. He prepared awesome hors d'oeuvres and entrees at our nightly happy hours on the beach. He was a great storyteller as well. I don't know if he was full of shit or not, but he told of clandestine ties to the United States government as well as the mob. He kept our attention with stories of secret CIA spy posts and aiding in the rescue of the Marcos family when the Philippines government fell. On and on he went, chewing his cigar and waving his hands in the air. I wondered if he was here to hide from something, or someone. The boat being named "Incognito" suggested so. Later I would learn that he wondered what I was hiding from. I never gave any indication that I was on the run, but he was an intelligent man.

He held court nightly on the beach, entertaining the club members with barely-believable stories from the worlds of politics and big business. He said he had written a book, but was waiting for certain real-life characters to die off before he published it. He already had a ton of money from building and selling an airport in central Florida.

Questions about the project produced more stories about Big Sugar and yokel Florida politicians. He was an interesting fellow and I was glad for his company.

We got to know him pretty well as our stay dragged on for months. I had intended to stay a few weeks. Andi never wanted to leave. She was enjoying the very active social life, but her fear of the sea was the real issue. She had gotten over the fit of anger from that first day and we had returned to our flirty but still platonic relationship. I got lots of comments from the male cruisers about how hot she was, and how lucky I was. I never let on that we weren't sleeping together. I tried a few times after too many cocktails with Captain Fred, but she gently fended me off. Usually she steered me to my bunk and put me to bed. Then she'd take her clothes off in front of me before disappearing into her own bed. It was maddening.

Meanwhile, we had become perfect examples of why this place was called Chicken Harbor. Georgetown tended to be the end of the line for southbound cruisers. Either they got wrapped up in all the fun and didn't want to leave, or they got their clocks cleaned attempting to go further south. They stayed here all winter and returned to Florida in the spring, vowing to "go south next year." As much as I liked Georgetown, I really wanted to continue on. My mission had been derailed yet again. The ashes were the only thing that could convince Andi to overcome her fears.

"You're right, Breeze," she told me. "You've got to finish this. I'll go, but I'm still afraid. Promise me we'll be safe."

"I can't guarantee anything but this," I said. "I will do everything in my power to keep us safe and comfortable."

We made *Ashes Aweigh* ready for an extended voyage. I bought a used SSB radio so that we could get reliable weather reports. We took on food, water and fuel. I studied charts and weather patterns diligently. The Out Islands offered little in the way of services. We'd be on our own for many days and many miles. I wanted to take a direct route and make good time through the Out Islands, not idly lag around like we'd done on the way to Georgetown. We'd only hole up if the weather was unfavorable. The next big stopover would be at Luperon, in the Dominican Republic.

Georgetown had gravity worse than Boot Key Harbor in Marathon, but we were finally breaking free. We said our goodbyes to the folks at the

RSYTC, with a special visit to *Incognito* to bid our farewells to Captain Fred.

"I'm going to miss you two," he said. "Andi has improved the scenery around here tenfold, and I'm grateful for the intelligent conversation."

I shook his hand and Andi gave him a peck on the cheek.

"We'll miss you too, Fred," I said. "It's been a pleasure."

"You keep the little lady safe out there, Breeze, or I'll come find you."

THE OUT ISLANDS

WITH THAT WE WERE GONE. I was chomping at the bit to get underway. We left Chicken Harbor in our wake and made way for Salt Pond. The trip was fine and Andi was relieved when we dropped anchor. I hoped she would regain her sea legs quickly. I spent hours poring over weather information, before happy hour interrupted my study. We took our drinks on the aft deck and held hands as the sun went down. It was good to be back at sea.

With a close eye on weather conditions, we took early morning departures and made mid-day landfalls at Calabash Bay and Conception. These islands were beautiful and isolated. The water was postcard clear. Andi returned to wearing bikinis or nothing at all, which suited me fine. I was surrounded by beauty. At the same time, there was an eerie feeling about these places. There was no safety net. We were as removed from civilization as we could be. I kept watching for pirate ships to appear on the horizon.

On the next good-weather day we made the jump to Rum Cay. We anchored off Port Nelson, which surprisingly had no port at all. We felt exposed in the open anchorage. We walked the sand streets of the settlement. It was like a trip back in time. I imagined that all of the Bahamas once looked like this. There were no hotels, casinos or cruise ships that crowded so much of the other islands.

On our next leg we made it to Mayaguana. We approached Abrahams Bay via the Guano Point Pass. I could see a well-defined break in the reef and passed through without difficulty. Then I could see another reef, which I hadn't expected. I slowed to a crawl. The water looked deep on either side of it. I tried to leave this second reef to port and pass between it and the point. That was a mistake. What I thought was the channel dead-ended into even more reef. I had to halt abruptly, back up and turn around. I carried a course that would leave the reef to starboard and made it inside Abrahams Bay.

I dropped the anchor and explained my mistake to Andi.

"Hey, we didn't hit anything," I said. All's well that ends well."

"You're a good captain Breeze," she said, which lifted my spirits some. "I trust you."

We took the tender towards a concrete dock that jutted out into the bay. We ran aground before we could reach it. I had to tilt the tender's motor up and get out and tow. Andi looked like Cleopatra on her throne as I struggled to drag my load through the shallow water. It was a long, hot walk to Customs and Immigration, but we needed to check out of the Bahamas before departing for the Turks and Caicos. I could see no facilities and very few people along the way. We were advised that the commandant was unavailable and we would have to return tomorrow.

We passed the time by sticking our nose in a book. Andi was halfway through *Freeways to Flip Flops*, by Sonia Marsh. It was a story about a woman who took her family to live in Belize for a year. I was just starting *Happier Than a Billionaire*, by Nadine Hays Pisani. It was about quitting your job, moving to Costa Rica, and living the zero-hour work week. I considered it educational material suitable for my circumstances. As the magic hour approached, we put down our books and poured drinks. We took them out on deck to celebrate the sun.

That night we talked for hours. We relived our trip so far, both the good and the bad. We laughed about how much money we'd burned through. You only live once. We talked like we once had, when we were young.

"What are you going to do once this trip is over?" she asked.

"I haven't a clue," I answered. "I guess I should start thinking about it. Right now I can't see past the BVI. I've got tunnel vision."

"As you should," she said. "That's why I'm here, to keep you focused."

"Why do you care so much about me and those ashes?" I asked.

"It's my way of helping," she said. "Just let me do my thing."

Then she asked me to recall the silly dream that had brought her to Fort Myers Beach, looking for me. She hadn't told me the whole story. In the dream I was in trouble. I was in a bad place. It was her mission to rescue me.

"What are you going to do when this is over?" I asked her.

"I haven't thought about it either," she said. "I'm still trying to save you."

I raised my glass up high to make a toast.

"To our missions," I said. "May we both find success."

The next day we again walked the sandy trail to attempt to check out of the country. We handed our passports and ship's papers to the commandant in a small, dusty shack. He took too much time examining them. Something didn't feel right. There was a problem with my passport. *Shit*. When we checked into the Bahamas way back in Bimini, a red flag must have gone up somewhere. Whatever paper pusher back in the United States saw that I had left the county would have no idea where I was going from there, but now they could know exactly where I was. The commandant asked that our vessel remain in the harbor at anchor until the issue was cleared up. Back on board I quickly checked on the weather. The forecast was not promising. We should have waited, but we could not.

Andi expressed her dissatisfaction with this new development. She had learned a bit about passage making. She knew this was a risky move. Leaving at mid-day would expose us to strong trade winds out in open water. I pointed out the small launch with the commandant aboard being rowed in our direction. We had no choice. I fired up the twin diesels and pulled up anchor in record time. We skirted the reefs on the way out at full throttle, another not-so-smart maneuver.

I couldn't believe it. Mayaguana is somewhere close to the end of the Earth. My issues with The Man were not over, even here close to a thousand miles away. My past misdeeds were still following me. On top of that, I was pushing *Ashes Aweigh* out into big, blue water. We could anticipate winds from twenty to twenty-five knots and nasty seas. I had broken my promise. It was going to be a rough ride and Andi wouldn't be pleased. *Good going Breeze.*

We beat and bashed through it. It was uncomfortable for a large portion of the trip, but I never felt in danger. My shipmate shot me that look again whenever we hit a particularly rough patch. Fifty nautical miles later it smoothed out a little as we entered the lee of Providenciales, Turks and Caicos. I navigated Sandbore Channel with no trouble and we dropped anchor in Sapodilla

Bay. We did not go to shore to visit Customs and Immigration. This was a likely stop for us after Mayaguana. I didn't want to show my passport.

We left at first light to cross the Caicos Bank. I was nervous about it. It had to be crossed during daylight hours. The whole bank averaged only eight feet of water with numerous coral heads and shoals. It was no place to run aground. I couldn't motor too fast either. We needed to pick our way through assorted obstacles. I wanted to see, identify and steer around anything even remotely suspicious. It took us all day. The colors, clarity and warmth of the bank waters were unbelievable. The reefs were pristine. The beaches looked to die for. I thought maybe we could explore this paradise more thoroughly on the way back, after the job was done. We finally anchored off Big Sand Cay. We were late for happy hour again.

I didn't feel particularly happy about this latest development, but that's was all the more reason to have a drink or six. We pondered our next move over rum drinks. I needed to get a real good look at the weather before we could continue. There was over eighty miles of open water between us and Luperon. How we would handle Customs in the

Dominican Republic I didn't know. It was a third-world country: maybe we could bribe our way in.

The weather forecast was iffy. We could make it, but marginal odds weren't good enough. After smashing south from Mayaguana to Provo, I couldn't force Andi out into rough waters again so soon. The anchorage was pretty nice, although a bit rolly. Holding appeared to be good in deep sand. The beach looked inviting, but I didn't want to leave the boat. I couldn't chance some park ranger or local authority showing up with a picture of *Ashes Aweigh*, looking for a runaway American.

We waited out the weather just relaxing and enjoying the scenery. I *read Key West: Tequila, a Pinch of Salt and a Quirky Slice of America*, by Jon Breakfield. It was about a couple from the UK who overstayed their visa and lived illegally in Key West. I figured I'd be living in the US illegally someday. I'd have to reenter without checking in and showing my passport. Maybe I should just stay down in the islands. I needed to do some research on extradition treaties.

Finally we got a good window, or at least a fair one. The first three-quarters of the eighty-mile run looked perfect. The last few hours could get a little breezy. I hoped we'd be in the lee of the big island by then. We pulled anchor before midnight, shooting for an early morning arrival. All went well for fifty miles. The twin diesels were humming along at ten knots. The winds were ten to fifteen. The seas had a gentle roll to them. Then it all went to hell.

A front was collapsing down on us and building the seas quickly. The waves were striking our port rear corner, lifting our aft end and causing us to roll awkwardly. If I tried to turn to port, we took them broadside. I quickly abandoned that idea and instead ran with the waves. The following sea was more manageable. I plotted ahead on the GPS and saw that on our present course we'd overshoot Luperon by ten miles or more. I hoped the wind would be blocked close to shore, allowing us to turn to port and make landfall. It was not. The winds slid down the face of the high hills of the Dominican Republic and accelerated. I could beat us to death by turning to cross the waves, or continue on to a different destination

I didn't even try to buck the flow. We rode with it and ducked into a place called Isabela Bay. This was not on my itinerary and I knew nothing about it. We were just north of the mouth of the Bajabonico River. There was a low red rock promontory which stood out as the only variation in miles of dark sand beach. I dropped anchor directly in front of Hotel Rancho del Sol.

Before the engines cooled a small runabout approached. Nice smiling young men informed us that they were with the Coast Guard. A shot of fear jolted me, but I didn't let it show. They couldn't know about me in this isolated outpost, could they? They did not. Their mission was to advise us that we couldn't check in to the country here. We must proceed to an official port of entry immediately. I told them we had just made a rough passage from the Turks and Caicos. We wished to rest and do systems checks before continuing to Luperon. I promised to be gone before sunrise the next morning. I was granted permission to stay. I was not granted permission to go ashore.

We left at six a.m. and had a smooth, short motor to the entrance to Luperon's harbor.

LUPERON AND PUERTO RICO

OUTSIDE THE ENTRANCE I BROUGHT us to a full stop. I was confused again. This whole traveling the world in a boat thing was harder than I thought. The water coming out of the harbor was dark. I couldn't read the depth. There were fishing net markers and little private buoys all over the place. There were no official markers that I could see. We just hovered there.

Over the VHF radio we heard a voice hailing us. It was the Commandancia.

"Vessel outside Luperon Harbor, if you wish to wait a few more minutes, I will send a boat out to guide you in."

I gladly accepted. Then I wondered if it was a ploy. They could send someone out to see if this was the infamous *Ashes Aweigh* with the naughty American on board. It was not a ploy. A young Dominican waved to us and we followed him in without a bump. That was the first of many polite and pleasant encounters with the people of this island.

We picked an open spot among the hundred or so boats at anchor and waited. It didn't take long for a clearance party to arrive. Three men boarded and we exchanged pleasantries. One spoke fluent English and introduced us to the Commandancia and the Ports Authority collector. I offered them all cold drinks. When I handed the can of Coke to the Commandancia, it included five crisp hundred dollar bills I had folded into the palm of my hand. That was a crap-load of dough in the DR. I smiled and asked for expedited service. I was willing for them to look over the boat with a fine tooth comb. I wanted no trouble. I promised to be a model citizen in exchange for a cursory examination of our passports.

"If you have drugs or other contraband, I cannot assist you," he said. I invited them to search, which they did, finding nothing. I was very happy to have left all that dope with Terry in Marathon.

"You are a generous man," he said. "I do not wish to know your affairs, but I will keep an eye on you. Do not cause trouble here."

I promised to lay low. I promised to spend money in his town. He granted us entry. We were in the Dominican Republic. Our passports were stamped. I could only trust that he wouldn't investigate matters more closely.

Once we got settled, we went to shore to explore the town. It lacked sophistication, but appeared to have anything one would need. We found a hardware store, hospital, police station, fire department, school, dentist, and assorted markets and restaurants. We introduced ourselves to Papo, to inquire about fuel and water. We met Derek, a little Scotsman in town. He could take us to the waterfalls if we wished. I was heartened to see Ana's liquor store. We were dangerously low on booze. Everywhere we went the people were cheerful and smiling. Everyone was so friendly.

We stopped at a small building with blue doors called Laisa's for an early dinner of rice, beans, salad and chicken. They brought each of us a huge bottle of Presidente beer. The dinner tab was less than ten bucks. Two dollars was more than twenty percent, but it seemed a paltry tip. The meal was good, and the service was excellent. I left a five and I thought Laisa would hug me. We passed several more restaurants in tiny buildings and I wanted to try them all.

Although not particularly attractive, the town of Luperon held a certain charm. Existence was minimal for these people but they all seemed so happy. I knew a little bit about living on the bare minimum, but it was a permanent way of life here. I was living on an expensive yacht and tipping fifty percent now. Their happiness was infectious. As we passed fellow cruisers from the harbor they would also smile and say "good afternoon." It seemed like a fine place to be. Maybe I could settle here eventually. I'd have to come to some kind of understanding with the Commandancia.

Back on board we surveyed our surroundings. The harbor was more like a lake, well inland from the ocean and protected from every direction. Mountains, cliffs and high-rolling hills rose up around us. The smell of fertile earth and jungle wafted down the hillsides. Despite the hundred boats, it was quiet. There were no loud parties going on. I could hear no music or chatter from my neighbors. It was all very peaceful.

I went to the chart table to do some plotting for the upcoming legs of our journey.

"Put those away, Breeze," said Andi. "We are staying put for a while. This place is wonderful and I'm in no hurry to leave. That big water out there is no fun."

"It is nice here, isn't it," I said. "Okay, we'll hang out for a bit."

I was glad that she appreciated our visit to the town. I wasn't sure that she would. The streets were dusty. Some of the shops and restaurants were little more than shacks. We noticed very few choices for provisioning. If you wanted toothpaste, for example, they had it. They did not have fifty brands to choose from, only one. It was the same for just about everything else. There was nothing cosmopolitan about it. I would be happy to stay here and rest. The isolation of the Out Islands and the rough crossing was behind us. There was still a long way to go. It was time for a break.

We made acquaintance with some of the area's expats. Some had arrived by boat and found it too wonderful to leave. They stayed on indefinitely, renewing their papers every ninety days. Apparently it was a simple process, as long as you were a good citizen. These were mostly retired couples. Some of the single, younger men were just like me. They had run from a failed life, or the law, and settled here. Everyone was on their best manners. I was told the Commandancia kept a very close eye on the activities of the harbor. He even had some of his men patrol at night, specifically to protect the boats and their owners. Crime was almost nonexistent here, unlike other parts of the DR. The townspeople depended on cruisers to spend their cash.

We wiled away the days at a slow pace, enjoying the congenial atmosphere. We took day trips to the waterfalls and Puerto Plata. Andi enjoyed walking the streets for fresh fruit, vegetables and bread. She befriended Laisa. She also liked to stop and talk to Rosa, who ran a boutique in the marina. We discovered a most excellent tipico restaurant, run by Papo's wife. We found internet service at the Vanessa pharmacy. We took the tender out of the bay to the beaches on the ocean side.

Our relationship grew closer. We were almost constantly holding hands or touching. She began to kiss me goodnight before retiring to her own room. We carried on long, intimate conversations. At night on the settee, she would lay her head on my lap as she read. What we didn't do was make love. Other than that we were like any husband and wife. We spent all of our time together and shared everything. It was a special time in a special place. I almost felt healed, but I was still holding onto Laura's ashes. There was still work to do.

The end of our permitted ninety days came too fast. We had to decide to renew, or move on. We hated to leave this place, but with great regret we agreed to return to our mission. The Mona Passage loomed. Neither of us was looking forward to it. I made a visit to the commandancia to say goodbye and thank him for his hospitality. I praised the people of Luperon as I slipped him a hundred dollar bill.

"Give this to someone in need," I said. "Or your favorite charity or church. I may wish to return someday if you will have me."

"You are most kind," he said. "You have been a wonderful guest. You and your lady friend are welcome to return at any time."

And with that we were gone. We had a southeast wind at ten to fifteen knots and moderate seas. I hammered down the coast to Samana and tucked in behind Punta Balandra. It wasn't pretty, and I had run *Ashes Aweigh* hard. The less time we spent out there in the trade winds, the better.

Running the Mona Passage to Puerto Rico concerned me. The prevailing winds were strong.

There were rough shoals off Cabo Engano and Balandra Head. Thunderstorms were apt to pop up anywhere. We had heard horror stories in Luperon from those who had gone before. We also had a nice older gentlemen tell us it could be a cake walk if done properly. He'd done it many times, always waiting for the proper weather window. I tried to remember all he had told me about night lees and land effects. He warned me not to skirt the shoals, but to steer far clear of them.

I screwed up my courage and prepared to haul anchor. I had Andi read off the checklist for departure. I left Samana behind and hugged the DR coast to stay in the lee of the island. Well before Hourglass Shoal we veered off and entered the open ocean. We ran a course to the northeast until we cleared the shoal by five miles. A right angle turn to the southeast put us on course for Boqueron. I turned on the autopilot and tried to relax. I sensed it struggling with the strong current. Then I saw the thunderheads building directly ahead. I'd have to change course. Thankful for the power I had at my command, I turned east towards Isla Desecheo and picked up the pace. We managed to miss the storm, but the seas got rough anyway. We turned back southeast and plowed through them. Once we cleared the Tourmaline Reef we turned back east. We made the anchorage at Boqueron in one piece.

As an American citizen entering an American territory, I was required to check in by phone. I did not. We didn't plan to stay anywhere more than one day if we could help it. There were dozens of places to tuck in for shelter along the southern shores of Puerto Rico. We ended up using almost all of them. In Boqueron we encountered a raucous and loud atmosphere. College kids carrying on like there was no tomorrow. Bars and restaurants were everywhere. Key West had nothing on this place. After the solitude of the Bahamas and the straighter society of Luperon, this was culture shock.

We left the very next morning for points east. As soon as we rounded Cabo Rojo the seas smacked us in the face. Andi gave me that look again, so I pulled off and tucked into a cove at La Parguera. We'd only traveled a few hours. In the morning we tried again. We had three hours of navigable seas before the winds rocked us again. We sought shelter at a place called Gilligan's Island. It featured a blue lagoon with a fantastic white sand beach. I yearned to go explore, but decided against it. I wasn't legally checked in and the park was manned by rangers.

We managed only few more miles the following day. At first light, everything looked like a go. By mid-morning the winds howled. We pulled into Ponce in a state of frustration. Would we ever get out of Puerto Rico? I didn't like Ponce. We could see a Kmart and a Walmart. All the fast food joints that you'd find in the States were present as well. Across from the yacht club, a big party was going on. It was one busy and loud anchorage.

We hoped for the best, but our luck did not change. It was blowing less than twenty knots but the seas were nasty and confused. I had to beat a hasty retreat to Caja De Muertos, an island six miles offshore. We found mooring balls and discovered this was a state park. I could see the rangers up above the white sand beach. Five days in Puerto Rico and we had traveled less than fifty miles. The winds always blew east and the current ran strong. I was beginning to despise this coast.

The next day we made Salinas to find more Walmarts and a Kentucky Fried Chicken. It was a nice harbor with everything any American city might have. I sat and listened to the NWS report for the eastern Caribbean. I turned on the AM radio for broadcasts from St. Thomas and San Juan. This God-forsaken stretch of water we were trying to cross was blessed with a steady trade wind of twenty knots. Only at first light, for a few hours, was traveling comfortable. We buckled down and continued hopping along. We made Puerto del Rey, a few spots I couldn't name, and finally made Culebra. From here it would be a relatively easy jump to St. Thomas in the USVI. From there you could look across the sea and make out the island of Tortola, in the BVI. Our target was within reach.

Our morale, however, was low. We hadn't left the boat since departing Luperon. *Ashes Aweigh* had become an expensive jail cell. We were low on some supplies, needed fuel, and we were cranky. Every day had been a battle to scratch out five or ten miles. We started to hate getting up in the morning. Instead of sitting quietly and enjoying our coffee during sunrise, we were rising before first light and scrambling to get underway while it was still somewhat calm. In the Bahamas most of our trips had been downright enjoyable. In Puerto Rico they had become a disheartening chore. I had to promise Andi that we'd spend some time in St. Thomas before getting down to business in the

BVI. We'd have some nights on the town and get stocked up on provisions.

We entered the USVI at Charlotte Amalie, St. Thomas. The USVI has a free port status. US vessels don't need to check in coming from Puerto Rico. This was a blessing. We put up the American flag and made ourselves at home in the very American city of St. Thomas.

THE BRITISH VIRGIN ISLANDS

AFTER REFRESHING OUR SPIRITS FOR a few days, my thoughts turned to the duty at hand. We sat anchored a mere twenty miles west of Tortola. We were almost to the end of our journey. Our pleasure cruise had become an ordeal. It had also become more about Andi and I, and the boat, than about Laura. That thought saddened me and brought back a bit of the old guilt. Memories of Laura came rushing back. I replayed our life together. I tried to feel her essence. Andi came to my side.

"What ya thinking about?" she asked.

"I was just having a little trip down memory lane," I told her. "I am so close. Now I'm wondering if it was all worth it. Maybe we could have just made a life together in Florida, forget about the ashes."

"You would never be whole," she said. "And you would never be mine. You have to do this Breeze. You told me yourself you had to do this."

"Oh I'm going through with it, don't worry about that," I said. "I just don't know how I will react. How will I feel when it's done?"

"I can't answer that for you," she said. "I can't answer that for myself."

She left for bed without disrobing or giving me a kiss.

We finally had calm water for our passage in the British Virgin Islands. It was a sparkling clear day with light winds and low humidity. The air here had a crisp quality to it. It made you want to breathe it all in. I got permission from Andi to do a little sight-seeing before we finished the deed. It was a delay tactic. We took a mooring ball off Cooper Island the first night.

"This is where I proposed to her," I said. "I hope you don't mind."

"Do what you have to do Breeze," she said. "This is your burden to bear now."

We sat with our drinks to take in the sunset. We didn't hold hands. We didn't speak. I got no goodnight kiss.

The next day we moved north to the Baths. We frolicked through the watery caves and hiked the hill to the restaurant for lunch. That night we moved over to Nanny Cay for dinner at Pusser's. Moving onward we moored in North Sound, Virgin Gorda. Drinks at Saba Rock followed dinner at the Bitter End Yacht Club. The next stop was Jost Van Dyke. We drank painkillers on the beach at White Bay. Andi wowed the crowd at the Soggy Dollar Bar by sunbathing nude. We moved around the corner to Great Bay and had a lobster dinner at Foxy's. Afterwards the music pumped and the people danced and we got carried away by the Caribbean party.

We stayed way too late and drank way too much. On the boat we almost fell down as we embraced. We stumbled to the settee and shared a long, sloppy, wet kiss. I fumbled with her sundress, trying to pull it up over her head. She stopped me. She stood and stepped out of it, then removed her panties and bra. My God she was beautiful. She sat in my lap, and gave me a much more precise kiss, long and deep. Breeze Junior sprang to attention. Then she put a hand flat against my chest and pushed away. She stood up and put her hands on her lovely hips.

"Not yet," she said. "You're almost home Breeze. Just giving you a little incentive."

With that she spun and retreated to her bunk. I sat bewildered in the dark. I was all revved up with no place to go. It finally dawned on me that spreading Laura's ashes was the ticket to Andi's heart, and body.

My erection and I staggered down the hall looking for my bunk. I was like a blind man waving a walking stick in front of me. I hit the sack and pondered what was to come. What would I do when it was over? Could Andi and I live happily ever after? Is that what I really wanted? The questions went unanswered as I drifted off to sleep. I'd have to face all that soon enough.

I awoke to the smell of bacon cooking and found Andi in the galley fixing breakfast. She handed me a cup of coffee.

"How far is it to Norman Island?" she asked. "You've beat around the bush enough. You can show me the other islands after we finish this, if you like."

"Five or six hours away," I answered. "Have you checked the weather?"

"The weather has been perfect every day since we got here," she said. "It will be perfect today.

Let's get this done. We didn't come all this way to get drunk at Foxy's."

I really couldn't argue her point. I wasn't even sure why I was putting it off. The mission had been my reason for living for so long. I suppose I hated to see it end. Reluctantly, I agreed. We set a course for The Bight at Norman Island.

We took a mooring ball near the famous Willy T's. It was a floating bar known for wild parties and raunchy behavior. Laura and I had skipped it when we were here. On the beach was Pirate's Cove Restaurant.

I wanted a drink before whatever ceremony I would perform, so we sat at the bar and ordered two painkillers. The bartender looked at me funny when I sat the urn next to me on a bar stool. I sat and contemplated what would happen next.

"I'm going to have to do this by myself," I said. "I hope you don't mind. You've been such a big part of this whole strange journey. I doubt I'd be here right now without you. I would have quit when it got tough. I would have stayed in Georgetown or Luperon forever. I can never repay you, but you have my deepest gratitude."

"This is a big moment for you," she said. "I'm happy to have helped, but you were the captain. I still can't believe how good you are with boats. You were born to the sea, Breeze. Now go. Do what you have to do. I'll be here waiting."

I cradled the urn and walked slowly to the edge of the surf. I was afraid of the feelings that might be released as I spread Laura's ashes. I had to give them up, but I didn't really want to. Thanks to Andi, there was no turning back now. I couldn't disappoint her. I had come thousands of miles for this very moment. I was about to complete my life's mission. I stood ankle deep in the warm Caribbean water and looked to the sky.

"Laura, if you can hear me, I'm sorry. I'm sorry for screwing up my life. I'm sorry for carrying your ashes all over the world, and treating them as if they were you. I'm sorry for my feelings for Andi, but I have to move on. And I'm sorry for that too, but it's what I have to do. Please forgive me. I will always love you."

I unscrewed the cap and gently scattered Laura's ashes where the sea met the sand. Some of them mixed into the beach. The rest drifted across the bay and joined the Caribbean Sea. They sparkled like stars in the afternoon sun. The deed was done. I had finally let her go.

I stood there and battled my conflicting emotions. I still felt a profound sense of loss. Laura had been gone for years. Now her ashes were gone forever. I hadn't just lost her. I had lost my ability to love. The hope was that by letting her go, I could get that back. I looked up at the bar where Andi sat waiting. Seeing her gave me a great feeling of accomplishment. I had done it. It was over. I was not a complete loser. I had fulfilled my promise to both Laura and her. It had been a worthwhile endeavor. I felt redeemed. I let redemption wash over me. I forgave myself for all of my shortcomings. I was still nothing but a boat bum, but I was worthy.

I turned and walked back up the beach to the bar. Behind the bartender were shelves full of random knick-knacks left behind by tourists to mark their visit.

"Can I put this up there?" I asked the bartender.

"Sure," he said. "That will be a first for us."

He placed the urn on the shelf between a bowling trophy and a conch shell.

"Are you okay?" asked Andi.

"I'm going to be fine," I said. "Thank you."

"I'm proud of you Breeze," she said. "Thank you for letting me be a part of it. My work is almost finished."

I didn't know what she meant by that. I thought we were done. My mission was over. I was proud of myself too. Without her there, I would have had no one to share it with. No one would have known what I had gone through. A witness made it more significant. She also gave me the courage to actually go through with it. Without her, I would have stood there on the beach and given in to my basic instincts. I wouldn't have done it. I would have held on forever. The trip would have been for naught. I'd still be a loser.

I sat at the bar wondering what to do next. I'd just spread my reason for living across the waters of The Bight. When in doubt, drink. I ordered a bucket of painkillers with two straws. I led Andi by the hand to the chaise lounges at the water's edge. We sat and shared the potent rum drink until we were pleasantly numb. Later we ordered dinner in the restaurant.

"Eat light," said Andi. "I've got a surprise for you later."

I turned my attention to what she was suggesting. It looked like we were finally going to make love. After all the months we had spent in close quarters, after seeing her naked so many times, after holding hands and kissing . . . it was finally going to happen. I felt a slight pang of guilt, because I wanted it to happen. Physically, I ached for her. I needed to experience her body once again. She had teased me with it relentlessly. It had been the driving force behind succeeding in my mission. I had earned it.

When we returned to *Ashes Aweigh*, she wasted no time. She stripped down outside on the aft deck. I did the same. We stood there naked for all to see, looking deep into each other's eyes. First she launched herself into me, kissing me hard and squeezing me tight. Then she yanked me by the arm and almost ran to her bunk with me in tow.

She shoved me down on the bed and attacked me. She became an animal. She was a hair-pulling, skin-biting, nail-scratching tigress. She used her tongue to taste every part of my body. I was wet with her saliva. If I tried to gain control, she forced me back prone. If I moved the wrong way, she bit me. As she made demands, she dug her nails into me. She was a demon from another dimension. She frightened me, but it was so very hot.

I had been with many women before Laura. I considered myself a good lover. I took pride in tending to the needs of a woman's body. This was something completely different. This untamed vixen allowed none of it. She was in charge and I was to be obedient. I had never dreamed that a woman could dominate me in bed like she was doing, especially someone so soft and sweet.

"Who are you? And what have you done to my sweet Andi?" I gasped.

She growled at me and pulled my hair, forcing my head where she wanted it to go. I gave in. I let myself go and joined her on another plane of existence. We tore each other apart, ravaging each other with a hunger I had never known. Our sweat mingled with our saliva and other juices, drenching the sheets. Nothing was taboo. Nothing was gentle. I was pounded and sucked and clawed into a frenzy. We were shameless beasts, humping and clawing and biting like cats in heat.

I hoped that she wouldn't rip my heart out of my chest and eat it in front of me. I was so turned on by it I couldn't stop. I fought my way on top and pinned her arms behind her head. She fought back by biting my shoulder. I cried out in pain but held fast. I stabbed her with the biggest, hardest, meanest erection I had ever had. Her hands slipped free and she wrapped her arms around me and held on tight, giving in to me.

We thumped together rhythmically, our hip bones slapping sharply with each thrust. I drove deep, trying to break her in half. Her sounds were sharp screams in time with each pounding. I heard myself panting like a dog. Then I stopped. She screamed, "Don't stop. Please don't stop."

Instead I went down. I parted her legs and finished her with my tongue. She bucked and wriggled and finally screamed out in sweet release. As soon as I felt her spasms, I remounted and stroked her once again. Slow and steady this time, I tried to last.

She screamed again, loud and uncontrolled, then a third time. It was too much for me. I couldn't take it anymore. I exploded like a flare fired into the sky. My fingers dug into her shoulders as my body was wracked again and again. My own screams rang out in the night. It was an otherworldly orgasm that you only read about in romance novels. It was violence, animal rage, sweat and blood and hunger. It cleansed me in a primal way. Her domination of me had forced the real man I once was to return. I was the great and mighty Breeze. I was the master of my domain. I was the victor in an epic battle of sexual will. I had taken this woman, and she had given in to me.

Then I collapsed on top of her. I was spent and weak. There was blood coming from the bite on my shoulder, but I couldn't bring myself to move. I was no longer sure about just who had won.

She felt so small and fragile under my weight, so I gently eased off her.

"I think we'll call it a tie," I said, barely able to breathe.

"We both won if you ask me," she said. "I didn't know how you would react, but you were magnificent." Soft Andi was back.

"That's good, because I don't want a rematch. My body can't take it. Is that how you like your sex these days?"

"It was hot, but no," she said. "At least not every time. It was a test. You passed with flying colors."

"I'm not sure I understand. I'm gonna need a week to recover."

"I had to see if the old Breeze was still in there," she said. "Breeze always wins. He doesn't run or hide, and he would never be dominated."

I thought that over quietly, not responding. She had made me feel powerful. I almost let her have her way with me, but in the end, the old Breeze resurfaced. I was myself again.

"Breeze," she said. "I believe my work here is done. My mission is complete too."

PARTING WAYS

"I'LL DRINK TO THAT," I said, getting up and heading for the liquor cabinet. Then I remembered my special stash of Punta Blanca. My best batch of homemade rum had been aging for a year. If ever there was a time to celebrate it was now. I filled two glasses with ice and carried a bottle back to the main stateroom.

"I'm sleeping here tonight," I declared. "You're welcome to stay, but this is my bunk from now on."

"I accept," she said with a chuckle.

We sat in quiet for twenty minutes, sipping the smooth rum. I reflected back on our journey. In my mind I saw the pretty beaches of the Bahamas, relived the rough passages, and considered the return trip. There were many miles under our keel, with many more to go. There were also many miles traveled in my personal journey. I had climbed out of the spiritual hole I had dug for myself. I didn't know what the future held, but I was ready to face it. Andi had saved me. She had saved me from myself. I was grateful from the deepest parts of my heart, but did I love her?

"What do we do now?" I asked suddenly.

"I say we go back to enjoying ourselves," she answered. "Puerto Rico sucked, and when we got here there was too much nervous tension. Show me these islands properly, now that our moods have lifted."

"A most excellent suggestion," I said. "Enjoy ourselves we shall."

And so we did. We toured every island of the BVI chain, including Anegada. The sand was so white, the water so blue, we were in heaven. We ate lobster dinners and made sweet, gentle love every night. We never missed a sunset. It was the most glorious time of my life, but there was an underlying feeling that it had to end. I made a few inquiries about our future plans, but I never got a straight answer.

"Just enjoy today," she would say.

Eventually, we needed supplies. The only place to provision was Tortola. I called the marina and they assigned me a slip. Tortola Harbor was a mess. Huge cruise ships lined the commercial docks.

Chartered sailboats clogged the channel. Fishing boats and recreational boats ran every which way. We picked our way through the chaos and found our dock. I hadn't pulled into a slip in a long time, but the twin diesels and thrusters made it easy. *Good job Breeze.*

The marina was bustling with activity and noise came from all directions. Not exactly paradise, but this visit was a necessity. There was a grocery store next to The Moorings charter company that we could walk to. We loaded up a cart and commenced to restock the boat. The next day I planned to fuel up and take on water while Andi went into town alone to shop. When she returned hours later, I sensed a change in her. She wasn't exactly icy, but she kept her distance.

That night over dinner, I returned to the topic of our future. She came right out with it.

"I can't stay here forever, Breeze," she said. "There's a life out there for me somewhere. I followed that silly dream. I fulfilled my mission. Now I need a new purpose."

"It's okay," I said. "I once followed the advice of a Green Flash."

"I'm not joking," she said. "I ran away from life once to live in Vermont. It wasn't the answer.

I'm smart and talented, more than just a pretty package. I have something to offer the world. I need to go back to the States."

"We can leave tomorrow," I said. "The boat is fueled up and ready to go."

"I'm not sure I'm looking forward to that," she said. "The trip here was so exciting. Chasing the holy grail, tilting at windmills and all that. Going back will just be grueling."

I thought the same, but I hadn't really planned anything after getting those ashes spread. I fantasized about a happy life together, but I hadn't done anything about it. I hadn't told her I loved her. I hadn't begged her to stay with me. Why not? She got up from her chair and walked around the table. She bent down and kissed me on the forehead.

"I love you, Meade Breeze. I will always love you."

Then she turned and walked away. I tried to answer her, but the words wouldn't come. I heard the door to the guest stateroom close. I cleaned up the dishes and went to bed alone.

When I awoke the next morning she was gone. I found a letter she had taped to the coffee pot. She knew that would be the first place I would go.

Dearest Breeze,

Please forgive me, but I couldn't face you. I couldn't stay with you or travel back home with you. I've taken the first flight out to return on my own. I will find my own destiny. Please don't look for me.

You don't love me, Breeze. Not like you loved Laura. Not even like you love that old boat. You have a great capacity for love still in you, but it is not for me. I hope you understand. You have renewed my faith in love. I see that it is a real thing. You've shown me that it is possible to love someone with all of your soul. I hope to find that for myself someday.

I will be forever grateful to you. You've shown me a life that I'll never forget.

Love Always,

Andi

P.S. Most of the money remains in my bank account. I left you as much as your coffee can would hold. It should be enough for food and fuel on your journey back. Sell Ashes Aweigh *and you'll be fine.*

I was stunned. I read it three times. I checked the coffee can. It was stuffed with hundreds. I didn't count it. It didn't matter. She was right. I had known real love once. I had known a deeply intimate, soul-sharing love with Laura. I didn't feel the same way about Andi. I was enamored with her beauty. Being with her was a tremendous boost to my ego. I was in love with the idea of her, but it was a mirage. We were special friends. We cared for each other deeply, but I couldn't deny that she was right. I didn't really love her.

Once again, she had proven to be the smarter one. She saved me a lot of pain by just pulling the bandage off all at once. She was gone, but I was going to be okay. She came, she saved me, and she left. I could only be thankful.

RETURN TRIP

I HAD IT ALL ONCE, AND lost it. I got it all back only to lose it again. I was not beaten though. Andi had restored me. I had this fine vessel, which I would sell. I had *Leap of Faith*, waiting for me in Marathon. I was going to be okay. I just needed to get back home, sell this boat and reunite with *Miss Leap*. It was time to go.

I counted the money. It was going to be close, but it should be enough. I spent some of it to change the oil in the twin diesels. I ran through all the system checks that had been ignored for weeks. I surveyed the food stores. We had bought enough food to last two people for several months. The booze situation was the same. I had plenty.

The only stop we hadn't made here was in Cane Garden Bay. I decided to stage there before crossing back to St. Thomas. That night I could see its lights, only twenty miles west. I sat alone to watch the sunset. I should have been sad, but I was not. The trip with Andi had been a life-changing experience for me. I was uplifted. Sure, I would miss her, but I wished her well. I raised my glass of rum and made a simple toast.

"To Andi."

I never saw her again.

The jump over to the USVI was an easy one. The first few runs along the southern coast of Puerto Rico weren't rough either. I had to tuck in behind Gilligan's Island again after a strong blow on day three. I could have continued, but it was such a pretty place. I wanted another look. I made it to Boqueron with no trouble at all. I joined the kids on the beach and partied my ass off. I brought a pretty little señorita back to the boat for a quick roll in the hay. It was fun.

The Mona Passage threatened me, but I didn't let it slow me down. I rode the east winds like a pirate, sloshing along at ten knots and ignoring the peril. From Samana I decided to visit Punta Cana. Three girls on vacation from Boston joined me at the pool bar. The redhead was sweet on me, so I gave her a vacation fling to remember. I was free and the living was easy, just like in the old days.

I looked forward to a return to Luperon, thinking I might stay a while. When I anchored in the harbor, the commandancia came out to me immediately.

"I'm sorry señor Breeze," he said. "There was word from the American embassy concerning your passport. I suggest you move on today. I will not register your appearance here."

"My apologies for any trouble I may have caused," I said. "I will do as you wish. Maybe someday I can return under better circumstances."

I had no choice but to leave right away. I couldn't risk causing problems for this friendly community. I couldn't risk being caught either.

This was not good. I would have liked to take on fuel and water here at least. I was going out into an unforgiving ocean unprepared. I'd have to find fuel in the Turks and Caicos, where I didn't want to check in with customs. My fears were well founded. Mother Ocean kicked my ass on the way to Big Sand Cay. The trades that had been on my port quarter on the way south, were on my starboard bow heading north. *Ashes Aweigh* got the shit kicked out of her during the crossing. I didn't much like it either.

The experience reminded me to be more diligent. I'd been a little too much like the old Breeze. Recklessness does not pay during ocean crossings. Sooner or later, the ocean will win. I sat down to listen to the SSB and devise a forecast. It was a go. I left the next morning and put the throttles down hard for Provo.

I pulled up to a fuel dock with my Q flag flying. Visiting boats coming from other countries were supposed to show a quarantine flag until they checked in with Customs and Immigration. I asked the attendant about procedures. I learned that if I did not go to land and continued out of the country, I wouldn't have to check in. I had my fuel and water. I made haste for the Bahamas.

I didn't know if the Bahamian government followed the same rules, but I used the same method through the islands. I left the Q flag flying and never went to land. I made it all the way to Bimini that way. I had to go in for fuel again, but I anchored off each night. I pushed the Grand Banks hard on every leg. I ran in rougher seas than we had on the way down. Not having Andi aboard gave me a bigger window in which to travel. I could take it rougher. The boat could take it. I still checked the weather judiciously, but I was the mighty Breeze, bashing my way from island to island.

The Gulf Stream crossing almost did me in. I thought I saw a running window in the forecast. It looked like there would be a five-hour period when it would be doable. I'd just crank up the diesels a few hundred extra RPMs and zip over to Miami. Those five hours shrunk to two and I got caught out in the Stream in wicked seas. The forty-seven foot *Ashes Aweigh* suddenly seemed very small. *Stupid Breeze*.

Towering walls of water crashed over the boat. She heeled like a sailboat whenever she got turned by a wave. I accelerated even more and crashed through them, trying to stay on course. I could see the Miami skyline. So close, yet so far. Finally the waves diminished to an almost comfortable level. I had exited the Gulf Stream.

I called the marina for help with my lines. The boat was covered in salt and who knew what else had been damaged. I patted her on the transom and said "Good job." I had pushed her too hard. She was a fine vessel, but I wouldn't be needing her anymore. Her job was finished. I was in a hurry to get back to *Miss Leap*. I tossed the keys to Dan-o on my way up the docks.

"Clean her up and sell her," I said. "Call me when you have a check for me."

He reached for his phone and called someone. I hoped it wasn't the authorities. As I hustled across the parking lot, a receptionist intercepted me with paperwork. With a sigh of relief I signed the contract and left her my number. I waved to Dan-o, took one last look at *Ashes Aweigh*, and walked off.

I was filled with anticipation during the shuttle ride to Marathon. I had a date with a very special lady. *Leap of Faith* was now the only lady left in my life. I had one travel bag full of clothes, and my trusty backpack with a coffee can of cash inside. There was nearly twenty grand left.

A NEW LEAP OF FAITH

T HE SHUTTLE DROPPED ME OFF near the city marina. I was now just a few blocks from getting the old boat back. The thousands of miles ran through my mind. It felt like I had been gone for twenty years. I had seen a large chunk of the Caribbean and changed my life over the past year.

The picture of Laura's ashes drifting off the beach was seared into my brain. The memory of that night with Andi was felt deep in my loins. As I walked I considered my lot in life once more. I had enjoyed the highs and suffered the lows. It had rarely been boring. I had felt the love of two very special women, but now I was alone. Given the chance to go back and do it all again, I wouldn't change a thing.

I walked through the gates of the Marathon Boatyard looking for *Leap of Faith*. I didn't see her right away so I went looking for Howie. I opened the door to his office and he spun around in his chair.

"Got damn if it isn't the ghost of Breeze returned from the dead," he said.

"I'm alive and kicking, you New York guinea," I replied. "How's *Miss Leap*?"

"She was about to be sold to pay off your debt," he said, looking at the floor. "I'm happy to see you, Breeze. You got back just in time."

"I would have killed you and everybody involved in that decision," I said. "I gave you fifty grand. How much more do I owe you?"

"You said you wanted the best of everything. Wait till you see her. She's a brand new boat. Everything is fucking perfect. The owner had to pay some of the contractors on your behalf."

"How much?" I asked again.

"You owe the yard nineteen five," he answered.

"Holy shit, Howie. That's everything I have, if I even have it all."

"Sorry Breeze, but that ain't my problem. You swore you was good for it."

I sat down at a work table and pushed some papers aside. I took off my backpack and pulled out the coffee can. I counted the cash three times.

Each time it totaled nineteen thousand, eight-hundred dollars. I'd be down to three hundred lousy bucks, but I had no choice. *Leap of Faith* was all I had, especially now. I'd figure something out until the Grand Banks sold.

"Here you go, you thieving bastard," I said. "Now give me my boat."

"You're gonna love it, Breeze," said Howie. "Every swinging dick that touched that boat did a topnotch job. I watched every one of them like a hawk. We all took a special interest in her. You'll have the finest vessel in all of Florida."

He took me to a covered shed where *Miss Leap* sat under tarps. We worked together pulling them off. I stepped back and couldn't believe what I saw. Her new paint absolutely gleamed, even in the shade. Every little scratch or ding was gone. Her bottom was smoother than the day she was built. I propped a ladder at the transom and climbed aboard. The results of her restoration were beyond my wildest dreams.

Every square inch of her interior was brand spanking new. She was well over thirty years old, but she now sported the latest in modern appliances and amenities. The old settee had been replaced by a leather sofa that reclined on either end. The vee berth and side bunk had been combined to create a spacious stateroom. A walk-in shower with sliding glass door had been installed in the head.

I opened the electric panel to see breakers had replaced the old fuses. Every wire was neatly labeled and secured. I opened the bilge to admire the new engine and saw that it was also brand new.

"Once we had the engine and batteries out of there, I had the boys scrub, sand and paint it," said Howie. "You could eat off that bilge floor."

"It's awesome, Howie," I said. "You've outdone yourself."

There were new fuel tanks, a fuel polishing system, new water tanks, new holding tank, and well, new everything.

We climbed up to the bridge and I removed the canvas cover from the helm. There I saw all new gauges and electronics, plus some additional items. She now had radar. Then I saw a rocker switch with arrows pointing right and left.

"What's this?" I asked.

"I got you a bow thruster," he answered. "You'll have no excuse for bumping my pilings when you come to visit."

I was speechless.

I finished my inspection in awe. My tired old boat had been transformed into something better than new. Her original construction was incredibly solid. Her lines were classic. Now she had the best of everything. There wasn't a boat on earth that could come close, in my opinion. I wanted to hug her.

"When can you launch her?" I asked.

"That's all you got to say?" said Howie.

"I'm sorry. I can't thank you enough. The cost has absolutely killed me, but she's perfect. I knew I could trust you to take care of her. She is absolutely one-hundred percent perfect."

"That's better," he said. "Like I told you, everybody took a real personal interest in her. They're all proud of the work they've done. We even took her out for a sea trial, and she's full of fuel and ready to go."

I held my hand out. When he took it I gave him a good man-hug, patting his back.

"Thank you, Howie. Thank you so much. We can splash her tomorrow. Let's go get a beer."

"I'll buy," He said. "Don't want to spend your broke-ass's last dollar."

As we set out for Dockside, I had to laugh at myself. I was down to my last dime but headed to a bar. I needed to get in touch with Tiki Terry. Hopefully he had some cash for me. We found familiar faces at the bar. They gave me a hearty welcome back. Carol was not behind the bar, nor anywhere in sight. We took empty bar stools and Howie ordered two beers.

"Has anyone been sniffing around asking for me, by any chance?" I asked him.

"I wanted to talk to you about that," he said. "Two guys in suits did come asking questions. Told them I never heard of you."

"What about the boat? Did they see it?"

"We had her all torn apart at that time," he said. "Even had the name off the transom. No way they could know."

"Thanks man. Guess I shouldn't hang around here too long."

"This about the stuff you find floating?" he asked.

"Actually, no," I said. "Old business. It just won't seem to go away."

We drank a few more beers and called it a night. I told him to take his time with the launch. I would catch up with Terry in the morning first. I walked back to the boatyard alone. I climbed up the ladder and again marveled at my refurbished vessel.

"You're beautiful *Miss Leap*," I told her. "We're going home. We're together again and we're going home."

As I went to sleep in my new bed, I had one fervent hope. Terry had to come through for me. If there was no money there, I'd be starving in a month. Two years ago I had been broke. One year ago I had two million dollars. Now I was broke again. *Brilliant Breeze.*

The meeting with Terry went pretty well. We dispensed with our greetings and pleasantries and got down to business.

"I sold half of it," he said. "Me and Troy and the girls smoked the rest of it, but I'll pay for it. Pretty good stuff. We all like it. When can we get some more?"

It looked like I was going back into the pot farming business. What choice did I have?

"So how much?" I asked. "I'm sort of in a jam."

"The half I sold brought fifteen hundred," he said. "So three grand is fair. Hope that helps."

"That's great, Terry," I said. "That will help a lot. Thanks."

He slid me the cash and we said our goodbyes. It would be months before I'd have a crop to bring in, if everything went well. I walked back to the boatyard in time to see Howie's boys putting *Leap of Faith* on the lift. Out of the shed and in the sunlight she really shined. Once she was in the water, I had them leave the slings under her while I did my checks. There was no water around the thru-hulls. The stuffing box was likewise dry. I checked the oil and coolant. I verified the water level in the batteries.

"What the hell?" growled Howie. "We done all that stuff already."

"I know, I know," I said. "Some things a man's just got to do for himself."

I finished up my inspection and gave a thumbs-up to the lift operator. I fired up the new diesel and listened to its sounds. I watched all the gauges go to normal operating levels. I looked down from the bridge and saw thirty or more guys standing on the dock next to the lift.

"This is most everybody that worked on her, Breeze," said Howie. "We all wanted to give her a send-off."

I climbed back down and onto the dock. I shook the hand of each man standing there. I thanked them all one by one. When I got to Howie I thought I saw moisture around his eyes.

"You bring that tub in here all wrecked up again, I'll kick your ass."

"I'll try to take care of her as well as you have old man," I said. "Thanks again for taking every penny I had."

That was enough of the goodbyes for me. I climbed back up the bridge and took the helm. The slings were pulled and we floated free. I backed her up then used the bow thruster to spin her and pointed for the channel. I couldn't wait to use the new autopilot once we cleared Boot Key Harbor.

I ran her up to eighteen hundred RPMs and the new engine growled. We were doing eight knots. I backed it down two hundred RPMs and it started to purr. That was her sweet spot. We made seven knots as we passed under the seven-mile bridge and into Florida Bay.

"This is it *Miss Leap*," I said aloud. "Breeze is back."

GOING HOME

JUST NORTH OF THE BRIDGE there's a winding channel with shoal water on both sides. Once I navigated that I could engage the autopilot. It was a straight shot to wherever I wanted to go. The Gulf of Mexico and the west coast of Florida was tame compared to most of the passages I had made in the Bahamas and the Caribbean. I decided on Fort Myers Beach. I really didn't expect for Andi to be there, but what the hell? I'd stop there just in case.

Miss Leap was happy. Her new engine continued to purr. She sliced through the blue Gulf waters with ease. Fifty miles out I let the autopilot do its job and went below to check on the engine room. All was well.

Out there on the Gulf, with no land in sight, I took stock of my situation. I'd spent three hundred dollars on food. I spent nothing on booze. If my still could be dug out of the mangroves I could make my own rum. I had three thousand dollars left in the coffee can. That had to last until I could harvest a crop and return to Marathon. I could make the round-trip a couple times on available fuel. I was right back where I had started. I was a boat bum, about to grow pot on one island and brew rum on another.

I was at peace with it.

Twenty hours later *Miss Leap* and I entered Matanzas Pass. We rounded Bowditch Point, passed under the bridge and approached the mooring field. It had always been tricky grabbing a ball by myself, but I had no problems. I was an old hand at this now.

I settled up with the office, took a nice hot shower, and put on my best shirt. I walked to the Smoking Oyster Brewery and looked inside. Andi was not there. I nursed a beer for two hours. She never showed. The next night I did the same thing. I nursed my one beer every night for a week. She never showed. I walked down to Times Square and sat on a bench watching the tourists go by. I walked for miles down Estero Boulevard every morning. I never caught a glimpse of her.

Finally I gave up. She wasn't there. It wasn't meant to be. I wasn't even sure why I was looking for her. I'd ask for a few bucks I suppose. I wasn't mad about the money. I'd let that go along with everything else. I'd sleep with her if she wanted to. None of it mattered anymore. She was gone. It was time to move on. Cayo Costa was calling me.

I returned to *Leap of Faith* and apologized to her.

"I'm sorry, girl," I said. "I just had to get that out of my system. I'm ready to go now."

I went through my pre-trip checks and let go of the mooring ball. Next stop Pelican Bay. *Miss Leap* and I crossed San Carlos Bay and ran up the Intercoastal past Sanibel, Captiva and Cabbage Key. I smiled when I could see Cayo Costa and Punta Blanca. Ussepa was off to starboard. The Boca Grande Pass came into view as I steered a wide U-turn towards Pelican Pass. I slowed to a crawl along the sand spit. The familiar confines of Pelican Bay lay before me.

There was one other boat in the bay. It was my old buddy Jamie Brown aboard Bay Dreamer. It warmed my heart to see a friend. I'd have to tell him that the gang in Marathon liked the dope I had grown from his seeds. He'd appreciate that. I might even have to ask him for more seeds.

I dropped anchor in the far southern end of the bay. Howie had taken the liberty of installing a new Manson Supreme anchor on the bow pulpit, along with a badass-looking windlass. I snubbed everything off and shut down the diesel.

"Good job *Miss Leap*," I said.

Dolphins rose to greet me. An osprey flew by with a mullet in its talons. A sea gull landed in the water off my stern, begging for a handout. I appreciated all of it. This was home. It was good to be home.

I had one last thing to do. I went below to retrieve my backpack. In it was one of those film canisters that once held pot seeds. One day back in Luperon, Andi had gone to the market by herself. While she was gone, I took that canister and filled it with a few ounces of Laura's ashes. I had kept that canister hidden ever since. That day on the beach at Norman Island, I knew I still had a piece of her. I would never completely let go. I put the canister on the dash where the urn used to be.

I finished up securing *Miss Leap*. I took the dinghy over to say hello to Jamie and Char. They gave me a few beers while we chatted on the beach.

I warmed a can of Dinty Moore Chicken and Dumplings for dinner. I'd be living on Spam and other canned goods for a while.

As the sun lowered over the Gulf of Mexico, I dug out the last bottle of aged Punta Blanca rum. I poured two shots and carried them out on the aft deck. I picked up the canister with Laura's remaining ashes and brought her out to view the show.

It was good to be home.

If only I could just survive until the Grand Banks sold. Until then, I was back to being trawler trash.

If you enjoyed this book, please write a review at Amazon.com. It really does help, and your feedback is greatly appreciated.

AUTHOR'S THOUGHTS

Trawler Trash is a work of fiction. I am not Breeze. Breeze is not me. We both just happened to attend Frostburg State, and play baseball. The real Andrea Mongeon died too young. The character of Andi is written in her memory.

My wife, the lovely Miss Kim, is and always will be, the love of my life.

Carol is not, and has never been, a bartender at Dockside. Howie doesn't run the boatyard in Marathon. Jamie doesn't have a collection of pot seeds. Art is not a dope dealer. You get the picture.

Captain Fred still lives aboard his seventy-foot Hatteras, *Incognito*, although not in the Bahamas.

Colorado Bob does like his rum, and Kentucky Tom is always short on cash. New Jersey Tom still has the whitest legs of anyone living in Florida.

ACKNOWLEDGMENTS

Cover design by http://ebooklaunch.com

Cover photo by Ed Robinson

Proofreading by http://www.jakelogsdon.com

Interior formatting by http://www.bluevalleyauthorservices.com

Contact Ed Robinson at kimandedrobinson@gmail.com

http://www.facebook.com/quityourjobandliveonaboat

http://quityourjobandliveonaboat.wordpress.com

OTHER BOOKS BY ED ROBINSON

LEAP OF FAITH; QUIT YOUR JOB AND LIVE ON A BOAT

They gave up everything and now they have it all. Follow them as they leave the working world behind and become carefree boat bums and beachcombers. Read how one couple got rid of all their belongings, quit their jobs, and moved onto a boat. This is a story of finding happiness in paradise through simplicity of life. It's tales from tropical adventures. It's a simple plan for financial freedom. It's social commentary on the state of today's society, sprinkled throughout with the lyrics from the songs that inspired them.

Amazon best seller in Happiness

POOP, BOOZE, AND BIKINIS

Ed Robinson's first book, Leap of Faith; Quit Your Job and Live on a Boat, was an Amazon best seller in multiple categories. Now he's back with this hilarious look at the nautical lifestyle. From Poop to Booze to Bikinis he covers the funnier side of the issues encountered by boaters of all types. With chapters like Signs You Live on a Boat, Stupid People on Rental Equipment, and Zombies Can't Swim, you'll find plenty of laughs. There's even a chapter for Tim Dorsey fans.

If you are a liveaboard cruiser, weekender, wannabe boater, have boating friends, or are just a fan of Ed Robinson's wit, you will enjoy this lighthearted romp through many maritime topics.

Amazon's number one best seller in Boating

THE UNTOLD STORY OF KIM

Best-selling non-fiction author Ed Robinson brings you this powerful true story of one woman's triumph over pain. It will lead you to hate doctors, lawyers, and insurance companies. By the time you finish, you'll have fallen in love with Kim.

This deeply inspiring tale is destined to become the most important book ever written about chronic pain and pain management in today's healthcare environment.

Amazon best seller in Pain Management and Physical Impairments

41755012R10151

Made in the USA
San Bernardino, CA
25 November 2016